I0104690

Exploring Ukrainian Folk Tales

A Study of the Polish Collections of Kolberg and Moszynska

Ukrainian Scholar Library

Exploring Ukrainian Folk Tales

A Study of the Polish Collections of Kolberg and Moszynska

Mykola Sumtsov

Translated and Annotated Edition

SOVA
BOOKS

SYDNEY

All rights reserved. No part of this publication may be reproduced, stored in a retrieval system, or transmitted in any way or form, or by any means, electronic, mechanical, photocopying, scanning, recording or otherwise without prior written permission of the publisher.

Copyright © Sova Books Pty Ltd 2025

Editorial Board: Eugen Hlywa (†), Mark Shumsky, Halyna Bondarenko, Natalia Stishova, Iryna Zorenko, Yulia Vereshchak, Julian Grodzicky, Mykola Garashchenko, Svitlana Yakovenko

Cover illustration: Andrii Kharlov
Translation: Svitlana Chornomorets

Series: *Ukrainian Scholar Library*
Book 4: *Exploring Ukrainian Folk Tales: A Study of the Polish Collections of Kolberg and Moszynska*

ISBN: 978-1-7637608-2-0 (Paperback)

In Ukrainian ethnography, Kolberg's collection of folk tales should be ranked immediately after those by Chubynsky (1872–78) and Manzhura (1890); in Polish ethnography, it stands as the most extensive compilation of Ukrainian folk tales.

Josefa Moszynska's folk tales are compelling from both historical and literary perspectives. Overall, the collection is remarkable for its content, completeness, and the significance of its versions of the folk tales.

Mykola Sumtsov (1894b)

Contents

Acknowledgements

This publication is the result of the collective efforts and support of many individuals. The driving force behind the *Ukrainian Scholar Library* series for many years has been Dr Eugen Hlywa, whose passing in 2017 marked a profound loss. His commitment to bringing Ukrainian cultural and scholarly heritage to global recognition lives on through this series and his writings.

We extend our heartfelt gratitude to everyone who contributed to this publication. Among those, we owe special thanks to the remarkable staff of the National Art Museum of Ukraine, particularly Yuliya Lytvynets and Lesia Tolstova, who selected and provided copies of Ukrainian artworks, some of which feature in this book.

We greatly appreciate the Polish Muzeum Mitologii Słowiańskiej for their unwavering support.

We are also deeply appreciative of the editorial board's exceptional work on this project. Their efforts have been invaluable.

Mykola Sumtsov (1854-1922)

Sumtsov: Scholar of Ukrainian Heritage

Svitlana Yakovenko

Mykola Sumtsov, born in 1854 in St. Petersburg, descended from Ukrainian kozak gentry. When he was just two years old, his father, a Kharkiv University graduate, relocated the family to Ukraine in 1856. It was there, in his ancestral homeland, that Mykola Sumtsov would spend the majority of his life and build his illustrious career.

Sumtsov had a deep connection to the Sumy region, the land of his ancestors. In the village of Borovlia, their family house preserved an inscription left by his great-grandfather, following an old Ukrainian custom: "This house was built by the servant of God, Semen Sumets*, on 2 May 1776."

Mykola Sumtsov received his secondary education at the Second Kharkiv Gymnasium, graduating with a silver medal in 1871. He then enrolled at Kharkiv University in the Faculty of History and Philology, studying under prominent scholars such as Kirpichnikov, Potebnia, Lavrovsky, Drinov, and Lebedev.

*Sumets – The surname Sumtsov is a russified version of the original Ukrainian surname Sumets, reflecting the policy of russification pursued by the Russian Empire. This policy aimed to assimilate Ukrainians by altering traditional Ukrainian surnames to fit Russian linguistic norms, often by adding Russian suffixes such as -ov or -in.

Graduating with a gold medal in 1875 for his work 'An Outline of the History of Philology', Sumtsov was retained at the Department of World Literature and sent abroad to prepare for a professorial position. In 1878, he defended his dissertation pro venia legendi 'On Prince Odoevsky' and began lecturing at the university. Two years later, he defended his master's dissertation on wedding rites, revealing his growing interest in ethnography.

His initial doctoral dissertation on Lazar Baranovych, focusing on the middle period of Ukrainian literature, was prohibited by the Russian Imperial government due to its critique of Moscow governors' actions in Ukraine. Sumtsov was forced to write a new dissertation, 'Bread in Rituals and Songs' (1885). By 1888, he had become an ordinary professor at Kharkiv University and went on to serve multiple terms as Dean of the Faculty of History and Philology.

Professor Sumtsov dedicated his scholarly efforts to the study of Ukrainian literature and folk traditions. His works appeared in publications such as *Kyivska Starovyna*, *Ethnographic Review*, and the *Kharkiv Historical and Philological Society Collection*. Active in the Society from 1880, he served as its secretary and later, from 1897, as its chairman. In 1892, he founded and chaired the Pedagogical Section of the Historical and Philological Society.

After the first revolution (1906), Sumtsov began lecturing in Ukrainian at the university, but this was soon prohibited by the Ministry of Education. Only after the second revolution was he able to resume teaching in Ukrainian. During this time, he published several brochures in Ukrainian and contributed an impassioned article to the *Russian Gazette* titled 'The Ukrainian Censorship'. He also chaired the University Commission advocating for the removal of restrictions on the Ukrainian language.

Sumtsov was an active participant in archaeological congresses and established an ethnographic museum at the Kharkiv university. Beyond his academic work, he devoted considerable energy to public service, co-founding the Kharkiv Public Library and playing a key role in the Kharkiv Literacy Society.

An esteemed professor at Kharkiv University, Sumtsov held numerous prestigious positions, including academician of the Ukrainian Academy of Sciences (1919), member of the Czech Academy of Sciences and Arts (1899), and corresponding member of the Saint Petersburg Academy of Sciences (1905). He was awarded the Great Gold Medal – the highest honour of the Imperial Russian Geographical Society (1916) – for his outstanding contributions.

Mykola Sumtsov left behind a remarkable scholarly legacy of approximately 1,500 publications. These works remain invaluable today and provide a foundation for further research in ethnography and the cultural history of Ukraine.

REFERENCES

Bahaliy, D 1923, 'Naukova spadshchyna akademika MF Sumtsova' [The scholarly legacy of academician M Sumtsov], *Chervonyi Shlyakh*, no. 3, pp. 162–171.

Kaminsky, V 1926, 'Etnohrafiia ta yii pytannia v pratsiakh akademika M Sumtsova' [Ethnography and its issues in the works of academician M Sumtsov] *Notes of the Historical and Philological Department of the Ukrainian Academy of Sciences*, vols. 7–8, Kyiv.

Lebedev, A 1909, 'Pervyi nauchnyi trud professora Sumtsova' [The first scholarly work of Professor Sumtsov] *Poshana: A Collection of the Kharkiv Historical and Philological Society Dedicated to Professor M Sumtsov*, vol. 18, Kharkiv.

Vietukhov, O 1924, 'Akademik M Sumtsov ta Potebnianstvo' [Academician M Sumtsov and Potebnianism], *Scientific Collection of the Kharkiv Research Department of Ukrainian Cultural History*, Kharkiv, vol. 1.

Yefremov, S 1926, 'Istoriia pysmenstva v pratsiakh akademika M Sumtsova' [The history of literature in the works of academician M Sumtsov], *Notes of the Historical and Philological Department of the Ukrainian Academy of Sciences*, vols. 7–8, Kyiv, pp. 1–6.

Introduction

Mykola Sumtsov

'Ukrainian folk tales in collections of Kolberg and Moszynska: as bibliographic materials on folk tales', a brief introduction by Mykola Sumtsov, was included in the original edition of his 1894 publication (1894b). In his commentaries on most of the folk tales presented, Sumtsov provides an extensive range of bibliographic references. A full list of these references is available in the Bibliography section of this book (see 'Bibliography' on page 161).

In my review of Romanov's *Belarusian Collection* (Sumtsov 1894e), I compiled an extensive list of bibliographic entries related to the Belarusian songs and folk tales it contains, occasionally providing comparative literary insights. This review, scheduled for publication later this year [1894] by the Academy of Sciences as part of the evaluations for the Makaryev Prize, is complemented by the present examination of two Ukrainian folk tale collections: Kolberg's Pokuttia region of Halychyna (1882–89, vol. 4) and by Moszynska's collection (1885) from the Kyiv province.

Mykola Sumtsov (1854-1922)

*The original publication refers to "Rus," which is (1) the historical name for Ukraine; and (2) one of the terms employed by Poland in reference to Ukraine and Ukrainians, up until 19th century.

Both works, dedicated to Ukrainian* folklore – Kolberg's focusing on the relatively underexplored Pokuttia region of Halychyna and Moszynska's on the native Ukrainian population of the Kyiv province – deserve thorough analysis alongside the foundational works of Afanasiev (1873 [?]), Chubynsky (1872–78), and other prominent ethnographers. Moszynska's concise collection, in particular, stands out for its folk tales, each holding substantial historical and literary significance.

PART 1

KOLBERG'S Collection

About Kolberg's Collection

Oskar Kolberg's *Pokucie*, vol. 4, 1882–89

The bibliographic review of Kolberg's *Pokucie*, published in 1889, might seem significantly delayed; such a review would hardly be necessary if the book were better known within our scholarly circles. Volumes 3 and 4 of *Pokucia* (Kolberg 1882–89, vols. 3 & 4) remain virtually unknown and unexplored, despite their valuable content. While the first two volumes of *Pokucia* (Kolberg 1882–89, vols. 1 & 2) have received some attention – referenced in M. Khalanskiy's dissertation on epics ([*bylyny*]; Khalanskiy 1893–96) and reviewed by C. Nejman in *Kyivan Antiquity* (Nejman 1884a & 1884b) – volumes 3 and 4 remain unacknowledged. A. Pypin included these reviews in the third volume of his *History of the*

Oskar Kolberg (1814–1890).

1. Mykola Sumtsov
refers to a series of his
articles contributed to
the Ukrainian periodical
Kievskaya Starina
(*Kyivan Antiquity*).
Titled 'Sovremennaya
malorusskaya etnografiya'
[The Modern Ukrainian
Ethnography] these were
published irregularly from
1892 to 1896.

*Yakiv Holovatsky (1814–
1888), historian, literary
scholar, ethnographer,
linguist, bibliographer,
lexicographer, and poet.
Member of the Ruthenian
Triad (Ruska triytsia) with
Markiyan Shashkevych
and Ivan Vahylevych. Best
known for his collection of
Ukrainian folk songs from
Halychyna, Bukovyna, and
Transcarpathia (Holovatsky
1878); see ill. on p. 66.*

Russian Ethnography (1890–92), highlighting the absence of volumes 3 and 4 of *Pokucia*. Similarly, M. Drahomanov's articles in the Bulgarian periodical *Sbornik za Narodni Umotvoreniya* (The Collection of Folk Tales] omitted any mention of volume 4 of *Pokucia*, despite its relevance to topics such as the analysis of the legend of the Angel's repentance [Drahomanov 1892, pp. 265–291].

This situation underscores the need for a bibliographic review of volume 3 [i. e. Kolberg 1882–89, vol. 3], to be published in *Kievskaya Starina* [*Kyivan Antiquity*], as continuation of 'The modern Ukrainian ethnography'[1]. A more comprehensive review of volume 4 (Kolberg 1882–89, vol. 4), given its larger size, which makes it unsuitable for *Kyivan Antiquity*, would be more appropriate for publication in *Ethnographic Review*.

When compared to the collections of Pavlo Chubynsky (1872–78) and Yakiv Holovatsky (1878), volume 3 (Kolberg 1882–89, vol. 3) – which covers *kolomyiky*, short songs, folk dances, beliefs about witches, local plant names, and legends about the creation of the world – is relatively less significant. In contrast, volume 4 (Kolberg 1882–89, vol. 4), dedicated entirely to the folk tales of the Carpathian highlanders, the Hutsuls, is of much greater importance.

Volume 4 is a comprehensive work spanning 328 pages, featuring 77 folk tales and 205 riddles. While the riddles are not addressed here due to their limited number and the need for a specialised study, the folk tales hold significant value. In Ukrainian ethnography, Kolberg's collection of folk tales should be ranked immediately after those by Chubynsky (1872–78) and Manzhura (1890); in Polish ethnography, it stands as the most extensive compilation of Ukrainian folk tales. Kolberg's reputation for meticulous and accurate collection methods is well-deserved.

His folk tales are accompanied by detailed notes on their origins and informants, with occasional references to related Polish versions in his other major work, *Lud* (1857–90). These references will be further enhanced here with comparisons to international versions.

This bibliographic work serves two main purposes: first, to acquaint local ethnographers with the rich content of volume 4 of *Pokucia* through concise summaries of the folk tales, potentially acting as a substitute for the actual collection, which is not widely known or accessible; second, to provide Polish ethnographers with essential bibliographic references, addressing a noticeable gap in notable academic publications like *Zbiór Wiadomości do Antropologii Krajowej*, and highlighting a broader deficiency in contemporary Polish folklore studies.

POKUCIE.

Obraz etnograficzny.

OSKAR KOLBERG

TOM IV.

KRAKÓW.

(Kolberg 1889, vol. 4).

1.1. The King's Son and the Chort's Daughter

The *Bida* [Misfortune] abducted the King's son and transported him atop a cloud to the dwelling of a *chort*, who had three daughters. The *chort* imposed impossible tasks on the King's son: felling an entire forest, draining the sea, ploughing a field, and sowing and reaping wheat – all within a single day. Each time, the King's son was aided by one of the *chort's* daughters. The eldest daughter enlisted the junior *chorty* to assist him, followed by the middle daughter, and finally, the youngest.

The youngest daughter and the King's son exchanged rings, enabling him to identify her despite the sisters' identical appearances. Together, they fled from the *chort's* clutches. During the pursuit, the *chort* transformed into thunder, prompting his daughter to turn into water and the King's son into a pillar. When the *chort* became lightning, his daughter transformed into the sea, and the King's son turned into a cross.

Upon returning home, the King's son married another woman, which caused him to lose his speech. The youngest daughter of the *chort*, meanwhile, hid within a well. It was only when the King's son encountered her again that he regained his speech and married her.

_^_

Comments: This folk tale reflects echoes of the classic Medea story, showcasing one of the earliest iterations of this archetype. Folklore often abounds with narratives involving impossible tasks and the supernatural transformation of lovers. A detailed exploration of these themes is available in *Contes Populaires de Lorraine* (Cosquin 1886, vol. 2, pp. 9–28, no. 32). For further reading on folk tales featuring impossible tasks, see:

Manzhura (1890, pp. 40–43);
Yastrebov (1894, pp. 130–134, no. 7);

Brautwette: Milch von weither warm zu bringen 5. — B.: Schloß und Goldweg zu bauen 9. — B.: Wasser des Teiches zu holen 5 B. — B. ums Leben: die Prinzessin zu finden 13; a. großen Holzstoß zu durchbauen, b. von zwei vollen Bechern reitend keinen Tropfen zu verschütten, c. mit der Braut als Mohr zu kämpfen 22. — ums Leben: Getreide auszulesen, die Prinzessin unter vielen zu erkennen, Lebenswasser zu holen 37. — B. ums Leben: 99 Hasen zu hüten (Gr. Nr. 165), Prinzessin auszufischen, Ring aus dem Meere zu holen 37 B. — B., über einen Graben mit dem Pferd zu setzen 58. — B. ums Leben: sich vor der Prinzessin zu verstecken 61. — B. ums Leben: a) 100 Ochsen und 500 Brote zu verzehren, b) im glühenden Backofen zu sitzen, c) gemischtes Getreide auszulesen, d) den Apfel vom großen Apfelbaum zu holen 63. — drei lachende Äpfel, drei weinende Quitten zu holen, dem Drachen und Besitzer der Bäume einen Zahn auszuziehen 114. — B., wer den Vater im Lügen übertrifft 39. — B., wer von Zweien das meiste Geld verdient, soll die Braut haben 53.

Hahn 1864, vol. 2, p. 323 (index entry under 'Brautwette').

2. Afanasiev – Due to ambiguities in the original source, it is not possible to provide a full reference to Afanasiev's collection throughout the text.

Chubynsky (1872–78, vol. 2, pp. 7–11);
Rudchenko (1869–70, vol. 2, pp. 153–156, no. 34);
Drahomanov (1876, pp. 290–292);
Afanasiev ([?], vol, 2, p. 297)[2];
Sadovnikov (1884, pp. 80–82, no. 14);
Ciszewski (1894, pp. 173–175, no 127);
Minaev (1876, pp. 95–98);
Luzel (1881) see notes under 'Epreuves';
Karlowicz (1888, p. 50, no. 80);
Ulanowska (1884, p. 317);
Karadžić (1870, pp. 208–211, no. 3);
Hahn (1864, vol. 2, p. 323) see index entry under 'Brautwette';
Chelchowski (1890–91, vol. 1, pp. 138–156, no. 22);
Maspero (1889, p. 229);
Kolberg (1857–90, vol. 14, p. 234); and
Riabykh (1893, p. 302).

'Medea Sitting on a Dragon' by Jost Amman (1599).

1.2. The Daughter and the Stepdaughter (1)

The Yazia-Zmiya [Yazia-She-Serpent] had a daughter and took in the daughter of a poor man to serve as her maid. She gave her own daughter delicate linen to sew, while the maid was given coarse linen.

The title 'The Daughter and the Stepdaughter' is misleading, as it concerns Yazia's daughter and her servant, not a stepdaughter.

When the Mother of God approached the Yazia-Zmiya's daughter asking for some linen, she was turned away. As a consequence, toads and snakes began to emerge from the daughter's eyes and mouth. In contrast, when the maid offered her linen to the Mother of God, precious stones fell from her eyes and lips.

The King's son fell in love with the maid. However, the Yazia-Zmiya deceitfully replaced the maid with her own daughter. When the King's son noticed snakes crawling from the impostor's mouth, he entombed her within a wall and set off to find his true love.

During his quest, he obtained a hat of invisibility, a covering-hundred-mile wagon, and a water-parting staff. The Yazia-Zmiya, who had been holding the maid captive, imposed impossible tasks on the King's son, such as felling a forest and sowing a field. With the help of evil spirits, he completed the tasks and escaped with the maid (Amaliya).

The Yazia-Zmiya pursued them, but thanks to the magic objects, the young couple managed to elude her and escape the serpent's grasp.

_^_

Comments: Kolberg connects the name 'Yazia' with the term 'jadowita' [żmyja; Engl., 'venomous snake'] (Kolberg, 1882–89, vol. 4, p. 8). The character may also evoke Baba Yaga, a figure found in similar folk tales. Kolberg included variations of this tale in *Lud* (1857–90, vol. 8, pp. 54–56, no. 22; vol. 17, p. 185 no. 3 vol. 14, pp. 80 & 81; & vol. 8, pp. 13–17, no. 7) and Wolf (1843, pp. 583–584).

Comparable examples include Chubynsky's tale about the Tsarivna, who produces gold from her mouth (Chubynsky 1872–78, vol. 2, pp. 27–35). The narrative incorporates common folk motifs, such as impossible tasks and magic objects. For further discussion of Yazia, see Afanasiev (1865–69, vol. 3, pp. 587–595) and Potebnia (1865).

1.3 The Daughter and the Stepdaughter (2)

This tale is a variation of the preceding folk story. In this version, the stepdaughter serves the Mare's Head and is rewarded for her efforts, while the daughter loses her life due to her rudeness.

_^_

Comments: Similar [Ukrainian] versions can be found in the collections of Chubynsky (1872–78, vol. 2, pp. 97–102) and Moszynska (1885, pp. 102–105; here see '2.9. The Wicked Stepmother and Her Daughter' on page 117). In Moszynska's version, the Mare's Head is replaced with a serpent [*Zmiy*].

Polish parallels appear in Kolberg's *Lud* (1857–90, vol. 14, pp. 30–35, no. 8; vol. 17, p. 186; & vol. 19, p. 240).

Russian counterparts to this tale can be found in the collections of Afanasiev (*Russian Folk Tales*) and Semenov (1893a, p. 194).

Illustration by Yurko Vovk for the Ukrainian folk tale 'Tsarenko and Zmiy', depicting Tsarenko saving the Tsarivna and slaying the Zmiy with the self-slaying sword(mich-samosich). The scene also features grateful animals: dogs, a bear, a hare, and a fox. (Vovk 1903).

1.4. The Magic Stone

An impoverished man traded his cow to an eagle in exchange for a magic stone that could transform into a table laden with food and drinks. He later traded the magic stone to a robber for a self-beating stick, which he used to kill the robber and reclaim his stone. Subsequently, he bartered the stone with a Gypsy for a cloak, from beneath which twelve soldiers emerged, and a cauldron that, when struck, conjured up a palace.

–^–

(Hahn 1864, vol. 1).

Comments: Kolberg includes Polish versions of this tale in *Lud* (1857–90, vol. 14, pp. 22–27, no. 6).

Tales featuring magic objects are widely popular and can be found in numerous collections, including:

Ciszewski (1894, pp. 168–170, no. 122);

Sarksiants (1892, p. 312);

Yusbishev (1892, p. 326);

Semenov (1893b pp. 11 & 85);

Piatirublev (1893, p. 169);

Hahn (1864, vol. 1, nos 2, 9 & 15, vol. 2, nos. 94 & 114);

Dobrovolskiy (1891, pp. 601–606, no. 32 & pp. 630–631, no. 38);

Manzhura (1890, pp. 25, 35, 45, 55, 62 & 77);

Chelchowski (1890–91, vol. 1, p. 105, 119, 240 & 241);

Minaev (1876, pp. 27–29);

Cosquin (1886, vol. 1, pp. 120–154, no. 11–12 & vol. 2, pp. 307–312, no. 75) and many others.

(Gonzenbach 1870).

1.5 & 1.6 The One Born Under a Lucky Star

A rich man spent the night at the humble home of a poor man, coinciding with the birth of the poor man's son. He overheard an Angel proclaim that the newborn would one day marry his (the rich man's) daughter.

The rich man bought the child and abandoned him in the hollow of a tree. A hunter later found the boy, who grew up to become a cook. The rich man hired him and sent him to his wife with a letter instructing her to kill the bearer. On his journey, the cook met a priest who altered the letter's message, leading to the young man's marriage to the rich man's daughter instead.

Angered, the rich man banished his son-in-law, sending him to seek his fortune. The son-in-law went on to heal the Tsar's son, who had been ailing for seven years, uncover a treasure, rescue the abducted Tsarivna, release a soldier from eternal duty, and ultimately marry the Tsarivna.

_^_

Comments: This is a well-known tale featuring Marko the Rich. For further details, see my research in *The Ethnographic Review* (Sumtsov 1894a).

'In Reshetylivka town' by Taras Shevchenko (1845).

1.7. The Power of Repentance

A childless man once stood beneath a bridge as the Lord passed over it with Apostles Peter and Paul. The Lord prophesied that the man would have a son who would ultimately cause his death. In time, the son was born, raised, and learned of the prophecy. Fearing its fulfilment, he left home, married, and amassed wealth.

One day, unaware that his parents had come to visit, he suspected his wife of infidelity. Mistaking his parents for her alleged lovers, he tragically ended their lives.

Overwhelmed with guilt, he visited monasteries to repent. Following the advice of a monk, he set himself on fire, leaving only his heart intact.

A Tsarivna later consumed the heart and became pregnant, leading to her imprisonment by her father. When the child was born and grew up, he revealed the truth about the Tsarivna's innocence (chastity) to the Tsar. As a result, he reunited with his wife and learned that, through divine grace, his parents had been restored to life.

_-^-_

Comments: Kolberg recorded a similar Polish version in *Lud* (1857–90, vol. 21, pp. 180–183, no. 4).

This peculiar folk tale merges two key motifs often found together:

(1) Parricide – Legends involving parricide date back to antiquity (King Oedipus) and have been thoroughly researched by Drahomanov (1891) and Grabowski (1892).

(2) The Repentant Sinner – The Galician (Halychyna) version of a sinner burning himself to death reflects apocryphal themes about repentance, seen in collections by Tikhonravov (1863) and Porfiryev (1890). For other versions of this legend, see:

Luzel (1881, part 1, p. 84);
Shapkarev (1892–94, vol. 8, pp. 105–108, no. 84);
Veselovskiy (1868);
Semenov (1893a, p. 199);
Sumtsov (1890); and
Zhdanov (1893).

1.8. The Envious Wife

The merchant's envious wife harassed his sister. In the merchant's absence, she first chopped up his golden cart and blamed the act on his sister. She then killed his best horse, and finally, her own child.

Upon returning, the merchant, believing his wife's accusations, cut off his sister's arms and cast her into a pit. The Tsarevych later found her, married her, and she gave birth to a son with a golden head and a moon on his navel. However, the envious wife told the Tsarevych that a puppy had been born instead. As a result, the mother and child were cast out.

In the fields, the sister dropped her son into a well, at which point her arms miraculously grew back to save him. The Tsarevych eventually found her and, in punishment, immured the merchant's envious wife within a wall.

_^_

Comments: A similar Ukrainian folk tale can be found in *Pokucia*, vol. 4, no. 10 (Kolberg 1882–89, vol. 4, pp. 49–53) [see '1.10. The Brother and the Sister' on page 34]. Kolberg also references similar tales:

Ukrainian – in Barącz (1866, p. 168),

Polish – in Kolberg (1857–90, vol. 14, no. 15, vol. 8, pp. 35–42, nos. 15 & 16 and vol. 21, pp. 177–180, no. 3); and

Dutch – in Wolf (1843, p. 175).

This tale belongs to a broad tradition of folk narratives and songs featuring wicked mothers-in-law or sisters-in-law, an archetype that echoes ancient myths, such as Amor's [Cupid's] envious mother in classical literature:

Comparable stories appear in:

Cosquin (1886, vol. 1, pp. 186–200, no. 17, pp. 255–257, no. 24, pp. 273–280, no. 28 & vol. 2, pp. 234–246, no. 65 & pp. 323–328, no. 78);

Carnoy & Nicolaides (1889, pp. 91–106);

Chelchowski (1890–91, vol. 1, pp. 156–166, nos. 23 & 28);

Maspero (1889, pp. x, 19–32, 200);

Manzhura (1890, pp. 33–36, 37–39, 49–50);

Afanasiev (1873[?]);

Benfey (1857–59, vol. 1, p. 254–269, no. 92);

Minaev (1876, pp. 95–98);

Karlowicz (1887, p. 246–247, no. 12);

Granstrem (1881);
Sadovnikov (1884, pp. 218–222, no. 65);
Hahn (1864, vol. 1, nos. 1 & 31; Cupid and Psyche);
Ivanov (1890–93, book 9, pp. 110–132);
Luzel (1881, vol. 3, pp. 31, 117 & 128);
Sarksiants (1892, p. 318);
Karadžić (1870, pp. 233–236, no. 11); and
Ciszewski (1894, pp. 120–121, no. 91).

Notably, Pushkin translated a Serbian song on this theme, 'The Sister and the Brothers' (originally, Karadžić 1845, pp. 38–42, no. 9).

1.9. The Virtuous Daughter and Wife

The merchant left his daughter in the care of an old man. When the old man attempted to seduce her and was refused, he wrote to the merchant, falsely claiming that she had run away with soldiers. Enraged, the merchant ordered his son to kill his sister and bring back her finger and heart as proof. The young man, moved by pity, spared his sister's life, cutting off only her finger and using the heart of a dog to deceive their father.

3. Drawing and quartering (also known as disruption or dismemberment) involves tying each of the victim's four limbs to a different horse, which are then driven in opposite directions.

The Tsarevych later married the girl. A year after their marriage, she gave birth to a son and set out to visit her father. On the way, a soldier attempted to assault her. In the ensuing struggle, he accidentally beheaded her child. The Tsarivna escaped, and justice was served: both the guilty old man and the soldier were torn apart by horses [3].

–^–

Comments: Similar Polish folk tales appear in *Lud* (Kolberg 1857–90, vol. 17, p. 180; & vol. 14, pp. 69–72, no. 15.

The motif about the severed finger is a common and recurring element in folklore, appearing in numerous folk tales and apocryphal texts about Solomon. Similar themes are widespread in Western European traditions, including English and Scottish ballads. For an in-depth discussion, see Child (1882–98, vol. 1, pp. 360–371, no. 41; vol. 2, pp. 288–295, no. 88 & pp. 373–376, no. 98).

1.10. The Brother and the Sister

_^_

Comments:

This folk tale closely resembles '1.8. The Envious Wife' on page 32.

1.11. The Substitution [1]

Twelve brothers married twelve maidens who, in reality, were not the robbers' daughters but their wives. At night, when the young men went to bed with the women, their youngest brother, Dzynholos, swapped their hats and kerchiefs: he placed the women's kerchiefs on his brothers' heads and their hats on the women. [Mistaking their wives for the brothers,] the robbers killed them. The brothers then fled.

The youngest brother, however, was captured. When the sole surviving robber's wife prepared to roast him, Dzynholos tricked her into demonstrating how to climb into the *pich* (oven), and he roasted her instead. Later, when a robber attempted to bury him alive, he [Dzynholos] asked him to measure the coffin. As soon as the robber lay down in it, Dzynholos threw him into the grave and buried him.

_^_

Comments: Almost identical folk tales appear in *Pokucia*, vol. 4, nos. 24 & 25 (Kolberg 1882–89, pp. 131–144) [here see '1.24. The Magic Horse' on page 48 & '1.25. The Substitution [2]' on page 48].

For further discussion of this folk tale, refer to the comments on folk tales 1.13 & 1.14, on page 36.

1.12. The Youth–Giving Water

Three sons set out in search of the youth-giving water for their elderly father. The youngest brother discovered the water and collected it in three bottles. In the first bottle, the water turned into a mouse; in the second, into a rat; and in the third, it remained the youth-giving water.

Entering a palace, the youngest brother encountered enchanted hay and grain (an army under a spell) and a maiden. However, his older brothers stole the youth-giving water from him. When they returned home, the father banished the youngest son and ordered his execution. The executioner, however, spared the boy's life, bringing back his little finger and the heart of a dog as false proof.

With the help of a mouse, rat, cat, and crayfish, the hero completed impossible tasks. He punished his brothers through exile and married the maiden.

_^_

Comments: Polish versions of this folk tale appear in *Lud* (Kolberg 1857–90, vol. 8, pp. 69–74, nos. 27 & 28; and vol. 21, pp. 175–177, no. 2).

For further discussion, see the comments on folk tales 1.13 and 1.14, on page 36.

'Podillia residents' by Leon Zienkowicz (1841).

1.13 & 1.14. The Insidious Sister

A poor man and his wife decided to kill their son and daughter. Overhearing their plan, the son woke his sister, and they fled. In the forest, they discovered a house belonging to twelve robbers. The brother killed them all and forbade his sister from entering the room where their bodies lay. Disobeying him, she entered, brought the robbers back to life with life-giving water, and fell in love with their chieftain. On his advice, she feigned illness and sent her brother on impossible tasks: to fetch hare, wolf, and bear milk, and later flour from the *chort's* mill. The brother succeeded and kept a leveret, a wolf cub, and a bear cub for himself.

When his sister and the chieftain plotted to kill him, the brother began to play his *sopilka*. The wolf cub and bear cub rushed to his aid and killed the robbers. His sister was executed[4].

_‸_

Comments: Similar Polish folk tales can be found in *Lud*, (Kolberg 1857–90, vol. 14, pp. 35–43, no. 9, pp. 113–115, no. 23, pp. 253–260, nos. 62 & 63; and vol. 8, p. 21, no. 9).

These folk tales (e.g., nos. 1.11–1.14) contain various motifs, including the motif of grateful animals.

(1) Grateful Animals – Tales featuring grateful animals are widespread. See:

Hahn (1864, vol. 1, nos. 9, 37 & 61 and vol. 2, no. 324);

Kazbek (1890, p. 83);

Knack's concise article on Greek legends about grateful animals was published in *Berliner Philologische Wochenschrift*, 1891, vol. 10, p. 37[5];

Carnoy & Nicolaides 1889, pp. 1-42, no. 1;

Cosquin's collection includes numerous folk tales featuring grateful animals (1886, vol. 1, pp. 166–177, no. 15; vol. 2, pp. 128–131, no. 50; and pp. 307–312, no. 75);

Grimm ([?] pp. 17, 62, 104 & 107);

4. In the original '13. Zdradliwa siostra' the brother beheaded his sister as her execution.

5. Incomplete or incorrect citation in the original.

Karadžić (1870, pp. 185–205, no. 1);
Sadovnikov (1884, pp. 28–41, no. 4);
Manzhura (1890, p. 16) [dog, duck and wolf];
Zawilinski 1889, pp. 9–21;
Minaev 1876, pp. 21–22 & pp. 29–30;
Kolberg 1857–90, vol. 8, pp. 117–118, no. 45;
Kazbek 1890, p. 83; and
Lopatinskiy 1891, p. 117.

Traditionally, three grateful animals feature in these tales, though the number can increase to five or six (Carnoy & Nicolaides , 1889) or reduce to one – often an eagle that carries the hero out of the underworld.

(2) Grateful Eagle – This motif appears in folk tales such as:

Cosquin (1886, vol. 2, pp. 135–146, no. 52);

Carnoy & Nicolaides (1889, pp. 84 & 85, no. 4);

Zawilinski (1889, pp. 28–38);

Chelchowski (1890–91, vol. 1, pp. 221);

Manzhura (1890, p. 36);

Karadžić (1870, pp. 185–205, no. 1 & pp. 236–244–205, no. 12);

Sanakoev (1890, pp. 182–183);

Toniev (1890, p. 196);

Hahn (1864, vol. 2, nos. 61 & 70);

Mochulskiy (1887, p. 140); and

Koropchevskiy (1874, p. 80).

(3) Life-Giving Water – The motif of life-giving water (or ointment) is common across various folk traditions:

Russian:

Afanasiev (1873 [?]);

Sadovnikov (1884, pp. 93–100, no. 18);

Ukrainian:

Chubynsky (1872–78, vol. 2, pp. 297–300);

French:

Cosquin (1886, vol. 1, pp. 32–50, no. 3, pp. 133–152, no. 12, pp. 186–200, no. 17 & pp. 208–221, no. 19, vol. 2, pp. 342–346, no. 82);

BIBLJOTEKA „WISŁY," TOM III.

Powieści i Opowiadania

LUDOWE

z okolic Przasnysza.

ZEBRAŁ

Stanisław Chełchowski.

Część I.

z zapomogi Kassy imienia Mianowskiego.

WARSZAWA.

Skład główny w księgarni M. AROTA.

Nowy Świat, 48 (róg Wareck. j).

1889.

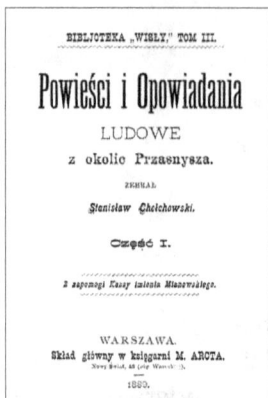

(Chełchowski 1890–91, vol. 3).

Luzel (1881, vol. 3, p. 470; see index entry);

Polish:

Chelchowski (1890–91, vol. 1, p. 211);

Zawilinski (1889, pp. 17-18);

Serbian:

Karadžić (1870, pp. 185–205, no. 1);

The Caucasus:

Sarksiants (1892, p. 316); and

In the Talmud:

Margolin (1880, p. 35), and many others.

1.15. The Robber and the Tsarivna

The Tsarivna was married to a robber. One evening, she arrived at his house in the forest while he was away. There, she discovered the corpses of murdered people. Terrified, she hid under the bed.

The robber soon returned with his friend, bringing a young woman with them. They cut off her head and removed a ring from her finger, which fell under the bed. The Tsarivna picked up the ring and fled to her parents, telling them everything she had witnessed. The robber was later hanged.

_^_

Comments: Numerous versions of this folk tale exist across various cultural collections. I shall refrain from listing them here, as I plan to explore this compelling motif in detail in 'Sketches on A. Pushkin', forthcoming in the *Russian Philological Bulletin*; work includes my analysis of 'Zhenikh' [The Bridegroom] [cf. Sumtsov 1893c & Sumtsov 1894c] a tale based on this motif. According to Smirnova, A. Pushkin was introduced to the story by his nanny Arina Rodionovna.

1.16. The Treacherous Tsarivna

The hero [of this folk tale] – a cabman – possessed a hat of invisibility, an indestructible shirt, an infallible shotgun, and an all-cleaving sabre. He married the Tsarivna, but she fell in love with a Moor, stole her husband's magical objects, and killed him.

A woman brought the cabman back to life. He transformed into a golden horse, but when the Moor stabbed him again, he turned into an apple tree, then into golden leaves, and finally into a drake. While the Moor attempted to capture him, the husband reclaimed his old clothes, executed the Moor, and punished his treacherous wife.[6]

'Tsarevych' (Lukashevych, 1909, p. 35)

_^_

Comments: This tale is particularly fascinating due to the ancient origins of its plot. A remarkably similar story can be traced back to ancient Egypt (Maspero 1889, no. 1). Among European peoples, the plot appears in both prose and song traditions.

6. The husband executed the Moor by shooting him and his wife by beheading her.

Similar Ukrainian tales include the stories about the slaughtered Brother the Little Ram or 'The Three-Year-Old Calf'. Other similar tales are included in almost all folk tale collections, such as:

Manzhura (1890, p. 57);
Khudiakov (1860–62, vol. 2, pp. 71–75, no. 56);
Sadovnikov (1884, pp. 218–222, no. 65);
Ciszewski (1894, pp. 89–97, no. 75); and
Cosquin (1886, vol. 1, pp. 60–81, no. 5 & pp. 246–254, no. 23).

Interestingly, a similar tale also appears among the Zulu people (Koropchevskiy 1874, p. 60).

1.17. The Zmiy-Slayer

The King had three daughters. When his eldest daughter became pregnant out of wedlock, she was exiled by her father. She took refuge in the house of a priest, where she gave birth to Vasyl the Tsarevych, who became a *bohatyr* at the remarkable age of just 13 weeks.

Vasyl the Tsarevych defeated Hryts Zalyzniak, who later formed a relationship with Vasyl's mother and plotted to kill him. Feigning illness, Vasyl's mother sent her son to the *Zmiyi*, hoping they would kill him; however, Vasyl defeated the *Zmiyi* and married the Tsarivna.

Zalyzniak eventually killed Vasyl, but Vasyl's sons revived him using life-giving water. In retribution, they executed Zalyzniak and their grandmother for their betrayal.

_^_

Comments: Similar Polish versions of the folk tale are found in *Lud* (Kolberg 1857–90, vol. 17, p. 183, no. 2).

The tale elaborates on the motif of the mother-traitor, a theme widespread across Europe, Asia, and Africa. Comparable stories or references to this motif can be found in:

Cosquin (1886, vol. 2, pp. 29–31, no. 33);

Khalanskiy (1893–96, vol. 1, p. 17);

Ciszewski (1894, pp. 89–97, no. 75; sister instead of mother);

Zawilinski (1889, pp. 28–38);

Manzhura (1890, pp. 37–39);

Sadovnikov (1884, pp. 67–72, no. 11 & pp. 133–134, no. 28);

Teptsov (1894, p. 18);

Eivazov (1894, p. 79); and

Schott (1845, pp. 262–280, no. 27).

'Yasat, the Priest's Son', featuring Yasat slaying the Zmiy. Illustration by Mahalevsky Yuriy (Rudchenko 1920a, p. 23).

1.18. The King's Daughter and the Shepherd

The King had a daughter who bore the sun and moon under her armpits. A shepherd named Vasyl traded piglets with her for the chance to look under her armpits. The King then proclaimed that whoever could correctly guess what was hidden there would marry his daughter, and Vasyl succeeded.

The King's daughter challenged Vasyl with a series of impossible tasks: to shepherd ten hares, to acquire a mountain of gold, and to kill the *Zmiyi*. Vasyl completed each of these tasks.

Disguised as a cat, Vasyl visited the *Zmiyi's* wives and learned their intentions: one, in the form of a pine tree, planned to freeze him; the second, in the form of an apple tree, and the third, as a well, sought to poison him.

The King's daughter then demanded that Vasyl eat twelve cows and drink twelve barrels of beer. With the help of *Viter* [Wind], *Moroz* [Frost], and *Holod* [Hunger], Vasyl consumed all the food, slept on hot iron, and finally saved the King's daughter from the Danube Rive.

_−^−_

Comments: Some elements of this folk tale are mirrored in a Polish version recorded in *Lud* (Kolberg 1857–90, vol. 19, pp. 219 & 226).

For additional references to folk tales featuring impossible tasks, see the comments on '1.1. The King's Son and the Chort's Daughter' on page 25.

This tale also incorporates the popular motif of giants, including *Obyidalo* (Devour-it-All), *Obpyvalo* (Drink-it-All), *Vyrvydube* (Pull-up-the-Oak), and *Vernyhora* (Turn-the-Mountain). For further details, refer to my academic review of Romanov's *Belarusian Collection* (Sumtsov 1894e).

The hero Boit-Tout [Drink-it-All] (Luzel 1881, vol. 3, pp. 301 & 308) is also relevant to this motif.

'*Vernydub* (Pull-up-the-Oak) ' *(Lukashevych, 1909, p. 71)*

1.19. The Shoemaker and the Bear

A poor shoemaker went into the forest to gather bast for making footwear. There, a bear challenged him to a contest to determine who was the stronger. The bear squeezed a stone, crushing it into dust. The shoemaker, however, discreetly squeezed cheese from his pocket, causing whey to drip onto a stone and tricking the bear into thinking he had extracted water from it.

The second contest – a running race – was also won by the shoemaker, who secretly had a hare run in his place, pretending it was his son.

For the third contest, testing the strength of one's strike, the shoemaker blindfolded the bear and struck its forehead with the an axe [its dull end?].

Afterward, the shoemaker made a friendship pact with the bear, and together they freed the Tsar's daughter from the *Zmiy*. The shoemaker, however, deceived the bear and married the Tsarivna himself. Furious and offended, the bear returned to the forest, vowing to eat the shoemaker. When it came for him, the shoemaker convinced the bear to place its paw in the split of a log, trapping it. He then killed the bear.

_^_

Comments: This tale combines several motifs rarely found together.

The dispute between a bear and a human over strength appears in many Russian folk tales, where it is often a woman who argues with the bear. Such versions are frequently indecent and have been published abroad (vol. 1 of *Kryptadia*).

The motif of squeezing water from a stone or crushing it is widespread in folk tales and epics.

The pinching of an animal's paw or the hand of a *lisovyk* (forest spirit), *domovyk* (house spirit), or similar figures appears in numerous ancient novellas and folk tales, including:

Stefanit and Ichnilat[7] [a Byzantine didactic work from the 11th–12th centuries];

German folk tales in the Brothers Grimm

7. *Stefanit and Ichnilat* is an adaptation of the Arabic *Kalila and Dimna*, which traces its origins back to the Indian *Panchatantra*.

collection (pinched beard ['Old Rinkrank' as well as 'Snow-White and Rose-Red']);

Cosquin (1886, vol. 1, pp. 28–31, no. 2);

Manzhura (1890, pp. 44 & 77);

Chelchowski (1890–91, vol. 1, p. 210); and

Living Antiquity, vol. 2, p. 163 (a Lappish folk tale).[8]

8. Incomplete or incorrect citation in the original.

Illustration for Brothers Grimm's 'Snow-White and Rose-Red' by Arthur Rackham (1917).

1.20. The Glass Mountain

In accordance with the terms of their late father's testament – who died after eating two bowls of gold coins – his three sons took turns guarding his grave.

The youngest son, Bailo, encountered a *chort* and flew away on it. During his journey, he saw the sun, which appeared like a mill wheel, and his father. Bailo obtained three hairs from his father, and with their help, he rescued the Tsarivna, from the Glass Mountain, and she became his wife.

The hero rode a magical horse, pulling golden and then silver armour from its ears. He later aided the Tsar, his father-in-law, in defeating his enemies. As a reward, Bailo inherited the entire tsardom from his father-in-law.

_^_

Comments: Similar Polish versions are recorded by Kolberg in *Lud* (1857–90, vol. 8, p. 172, nos. 71–72; vol. 9, no. 1).

The motif of sons guarding their father's grave is widespread in folklore. The Glass Mountain, the rescue of a Tsarivna, and related elements are also common themes, as discussed by Afanasiev (1865–69).

1.21. The Golden Bird and the Sea Tsarivna

The Tsar had three sons and a golden apple tree. Every night, someone stole apples from the tree. The youngest son discovered that a golden bird was the thief and managed to pull out one of its feathers in an attempt to catch it. The Tsar then sent him on a quest to retrieve the bird from another Tsar.

A wolf carried the youngest son on his journey. The Tsar who owned the golden bird sent him on another task: to fetch the golden horse. The Tsar who owned the golden horse, in turn, demanded that he bring the Sea Tsarivna.

'The Glass Mountain' (Wojcieki 1876, p. 155).

The wolf carried the hero to each destination. However, his two older brothers stole the Sea Tsarivna from him and killed him. The wolf brought the youngest son back to life. Disguised as a violinist, the hero appeared at the wedding. The Sea Tsarivna recognised him by his playing and chose to marry him. The Tsar exiled the two eldest sons and bequeathed his tsardom to the youngest

_^_

Comments: Polish versions of this folk tale are included *Lud*, (Kolberg, 1857–90, vol. 14, no. 22; & vol. 19, p. 234).

The tale incorporates several well-known motifs. For references to impossible tasks, see the comments on '1.1. The King's Son and the Chort's Daughter' on page 25.

The motif of the hero arriving at the wedding disguised as a musician (violinist) is particularly popular in songs, ballads, and epics about Dobrynia, which I analyse in detail in my article 'Husband at the Wedding of His Wife' (Sumtsov 1893b).

The golden bird's feather at the beginning of the tale serves as the source of the hero's misfortunes. This motif is common in folklore and can be found in the following collections:

Cosquin (1886, vol. 2, pp. 290–303, no. 73);

Manzhura (1890, p. 46);

Kosinski (1881 p. 252);

Sadovnikov (1884, pp. 73–77, no. 12);

Sarksiants (1892, p. 32); &

Eivazov (1894, pp. 72–78).

'Dobrynia' by A. Riabushkin (1895).

The plot of this fairy tale is widespread. The hero accidentally acquires a golden bird's feather – the source of many trials. The Tsar orders the hero to find the bird, only for him to discover that the bird is actually a Tsarivna. After a series of typical fairy-tale adventures, the hero marries her.

1.22. The Son of Shoemaker as the King

The shoemaker banished his son. An old woman gave the boy a stick, a hammer, and a key, and taught him how to acquire a fallen city – once a prosperous capital. The hero successfully seized the city and married the Tsar's daughter.

Following her advice, he obtained the hat of invisibility, the hundred-verst boots, and the self-beating stick. He marched to confront his father with an army, but robbers defeated him and his soldiers. Upon hearing of her husband's failure, the Tsar's daughter led her own army, defeated the robbers, and reunited with her husband.

_^_

Comments: Similar Polish versions are recorded in *Lud* (Kolberg 1857–90, vol. 19, p. 191; & vol. 14, p. 10, no. 2, p. 80, no. 18, pp. 105–106, no. 22 & p. 114, no. 23).

This folk tale combines various motifs that are loosely connected and insufficiently developed. The most cohesive elements are the magic objects, which are widely known from other folk tales.

The hat of invisibility, the self-walking boots, and the self-beating stick (or the magic shotgun) appear in numerous collections, including:

Afanasiev (1873 [?]);

Chubynsky (1872–78, vol. 2, pp. 358–359);

Manzhura (1890, pp. 55–57);

Dobrovolskiy (1891, pp. 630–631, no. 38);

Sarksiants (1892, p. 312);

Yusbishev (1892, p. 326);

Semenov (1893b pp. 11 & 85);

Piatirublev (1893, p. 169);

Hahn (1864, vol. 2, p. 165); and

Cosquin (1886, vol. 1, pp. 120–132, nos. 11–12).

For additional references to magic objects, see the comments on '1.4. The Magic Stone' on page 29.

1.23. The Merchant and the Tsarivna

The son of a merchant saved another merchant from execution by paying his debts. Later, he fell into the hands of pirates. He made them drunk, killed them, and rescued the Tsarivna, whom they had held captive, eventually marrying her.

When they reached the Tsarivna's homeland, the merchant's son carried her portrait. Her former fiancé, the minister, threw him into the sea. He washed ashore on an island, where the merchant he had previously saved found him and gifted him a magic ring that could fulfil any desire. Using the ring, the merchant's son returned to his wife.

_^_

Comments: In Western literature, similar tales appear in chapbooks. It is likely that this Ukrainian folk tale from the Halychyna region was influenced by these Western chapbooks, also known as *Volksbücher*. Another similar tale features the motif of a grateful revenant [*mrets*].

1.24. The Magic Horse

_^_

Comments: This tale is a variation of '1.11. The Substitution [1]' on page 34.

1.25. The Substitution [2]

_^_

Comments: This tale is a variation of '1.11. The Substitution [1]' on page 34.

1.26. Madey's Bed

_^_

Comments: See '1.28. Return of the Father's Promissory Note' on page 49.

1.27. Ivan the Robber

_^_

Comments: See '1.28. Return of the Father's Promissory Note' on page 49.

1.28. Return of the Father's Promissory Note

_^_

Comments: Folk tales nos. 1.26, 1.27 and 1.28 are variations of the tale about the penitent robber and the return of the promissory note. J. Karlowicz published an insightful study on this subject in *Wisla* (1890)[8], which includes numerous versions of the tale. As a supplement to Karlowicz's work, additional versions can be found in my article on Christian legends (Sumtsov 1890).

This folk tale, recorded by Kolberg consists of three distinct parts:

(1) The first part presents a variation of the folk tale '1.26. Madey's Bed' on page 48.

(2) The second part focuses on *chort's* impossible tasks – taming a horse and building a golden bridge – with Lucifer's youngest daughter aiding the hero.

(3) The third part features an escape and shape-shifting sequence: Lucifer's daughter transforms into millet and the hero into wheat; then she becomes water, and he turns into a drake. The motif of shape-shifting in this final part is common in other folk tales.

8. Incomplete or incorrect citation in the original.

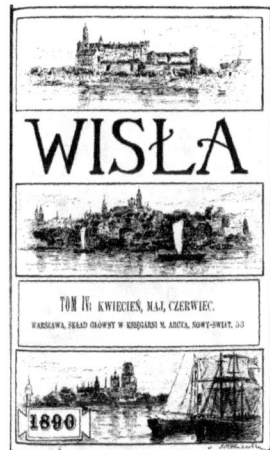

(Wisla, *1890, vol. 4.*)

I plan to analyse this motif in detail in a forthcoming monograph, where I will discuss eight intricate and fascinating forms of shape-shifting found in traditional legends, literary records, and oral folklore.

1.29. About the Young Man who Sold his Skin to the Chort

This is a demonological tale.

The *chort* gave a poor man money in exchange for his skin, which he would remove after the man's death. As repayment of the loan's interest, the man had to stand guard in the cemetery. There, he witnessed the *chort* removing the skin from a corpse and wearing it. However, the *chort* could not harm his debtor because the man's clothes had been blessed. The *chort* then walked around the village disguised in the skin of the dead man.

_^_

Comments: This folk tale reflects a popular belief in Ukraine that *chorty* dress themselves in the skin of warlocks, which can be removed like a sack by shaking the body out of it. Similar folk tales are recorded in the collections of Ivanov (1890–93) and Podbereski (1880).

Detail of I. Prianishnikov's illustration (1874-76) from M. Hohol's novel 'The Lost Letter'; featuring chorty.

1.30. About the Young Man who Feared Nothing

There was once a young man who feared nothing: neither the deacon haunting the bell tower at night, nor the dead in the funeral parlour, nor the *chorty* in the cursed castle where the Tsar ordered him to spend the night. However, a mere trifle finally frightened him – when cold water was poured over his head.

_^_

Comments: Numerous versions of this folk tale are found in the folklore of many peoples. Kolberg provides the following references:

Polish: *Lud* (Kolberg 1857–90, vol. 3, pp. 119–122, no. 3 and vol. 8, p. 133, no. 53).

Dutch: in Wolf (1843, pp. 431–432); and

German (a version from the Upper Palatinate) in Schönwerth (1858, p. 405[9]).

9. Incomplete or incorrect citation in the original.

10. Incomplete or incorrect citation in the original.

To these, we add:

Cosquin (1886, vol. 2, pp. 253–263, no. 67);
Manzhura (1890, pp. 60–61);
Kozlowski (*Lud* 336, 368)[10];
Vereshchagin (1886, p. 161);
Gonzenbach (1870, vol. 2, p. 237);
Hahn (1864, vol. 1, nos. 24 & 32 and vol. 2, no. 64);
Schleicher (1857, pp. 128–141);
Afanasiev (1873 [?]);
Shapkarev (1892–94, vol. 8, pp. 219–221, no. 122);
Ciszewski (1894, pp. 209–210, no. 154); and
Yastrebov (1894, p. 81).

This motif has roots in ancient Germanic legends about Thor and Greek legends about Hercules.

Niederländische Sagen.

Gesammelt und mit Anmerkungen begleitet

herausgegeben

von

Johann Wilhelm Wolf.

Mit einem Kupfer.

Leipzig:
F. A. Brockhaus.
1843.

(Wolf 1843)

1.31. The Miserly Peasant

A miserly peasant ate his money before dying. A young man went to the cemetery and witnessed *chorty* removing the money from the corpse and taking the body away with them.

_^_

Comments: A Polish version of this folk tale can be found in Kolberg's *Lud*, (1857–90, vol. 8, p. 172, no. 71.)

This tale is a variation of the preceding folk tale, '1.29. About the Young Man who Sold his Skin to the Chort' on page 50].

1.32. The Chort and the Bread

Eleven brothers married eleven maidens (sisters). Out of envy, a *chort* immured them and set out to torture the twelfth, youngest, brother, who had remained at home. The youngest brother hung a slice of bread on the door lock.

When the *chort* arrived, he asked the bread whether its owner was kind. The bread recounted its bitter fate: how it had been tortured with a plough, cut with a scythe, threshed with a flail, and kneaded in a kneading trough. Hearing this, the *chort* fled in fear and freed the eleven brothers, who brought back a maiden as a wife for their youngest brother.

_^_

Comments: The opening of this tale resembles the motifs found in '1.11. The Substitution', '1.24. The Magic Horse', and '1.25. The Substitution' [see pp. 34 & 48].

This fascinating story about the 'torments of bread' appears to have been known to Kolberg only in this Galician (Halychyna) version. Closely related tales appear in various traditions::

Belarusian: Romanov (1887);

Ukrainian: Yastrebov (1894, pp. 135–136, no. 10), where a spinning strand replaces the bread; and

Romanian: Kremnitz (1882).

1.33. How the Miserly Priest Became Generous

The miserly priest never gave food to his labourers. One day, while on his way to a ball, his coachman deliberately turned off the road and drove aimlessly for several days. The coachman had brought a supply of bread, which he ate discreetly, hiding it from the priest. Having experienced true hunger for the first time, the priest returned home and began feeding his people well.

_^_

Comments: In Ukraine, there is a version of this folk tale where *Pany* (landlords) replace the priest as the central figure.

1.34. How the Young Man Made the Rich Maiden Laugh

A young man earned seven grains, which were eaten by two roosters. Then, two rams butted the roosters. An old woman and a maiden attempted to shear the rams' wool but became stuck to them. When the miller slapped the old woman on her bare bottom with his shovel, both the shovel and the miller himself became stuck to her.

The rich man's daughter, who was always sad, saw the scene and burst into laughter. Her father, [delighted], married her off to the young man.

_^_

Comments: Kolberg cites two versions of this folk tale: a Polish version in *Lud* (Kolberg 1857–90, vol. 14, p. 233–236, no. 55) and a Ukrainian version in Barącz's collection (1866, p. 207).

The motif of people and objects becoming stuck together has roots in classical antiquity (e.g., the tales of Midas). This motif is also present in Caucasian folklore, as discussed in Miller's review of Caucasian folk legends (1893).

1.35. The Son of Bear

A she-bear conceived a son with a priest in the forest, and the child later became the priest's labourer. The labourer brought a she-bear from the forest, which crushed the priest's oxen. He then killed the priest's child, drowned the priest's wife, and travelled with a Gypsy, tricking a widow's lover by fooling him into kissing his bottom.

_^_

Comments: Numerous versions of this folk tale exist, and most omit the indecent ending. These versions are often known by alternate titles such as 'About the Priest's Hireling', 'About the Labourer-Strongman', or more often 'About Medvidko'.

Ukrainian versions of this tale are found in Moszynska (1885, pp. 152–155, nos. 32 & 33) [here see '2.32. About Ivan the Priest's Hireling' on page 148 & '2.33. About the Priest's Hireling' on page 148]; Polish versions appear in *Lud* (Kolberg 1857–90, vol. 14, p. 116, no. 24 & p. 220, no. 50 and vol. 15, pp. 295 & 296).

Oleksandr Potebnia (1835–1891), Ukrainian linguist, ethnographer, and philosopher, whose works on language, folklore, and thought processes remain foundational in Slavic studies.

The motif of the Son of Bear or the Son of Mare who grows up to become a *bohatyr* is found in:
Cosquin (1886, vol. 1, pp. 1–27, no. 1);
Manzhura (1890, pp. 43–45);
Vereshchagin (1886, p. 133);
Potebnia (1881, p. 80);
Karadžić (1870, pp. 1–7, no. 1);
Shapkarev (1892–94, vol. 8, pp. 333–335, no. 191);
Sadovnikov (1884, p. 150, no. 34);
Khudiakov (1860–62, vol. 2, pp. 43–46, no. 46; Ivan, the Son of Cat);
Potanin (1881–83, issue 2, pp. 161–163, no. 19; donkey, pig and bull);
Toniev (1890, p. 189);
Mashurko (1894, pp. 388–402);
Dobrovolskiy (1891, pp. 410–416, no. 6 (cow) & pp. 416–433, no. 7 (dog); and
Hahn 1864, vol. 1, no. 14 (goats), nos. 31 & 41 & 100 (snakes).

1.36. The Unfaithful Wife and the Vovkulaka

The priest's wife had a love affair with a Gypsy. While the priest's labourer, who was a *znakhar* (folk healer), was ploughing the field, he informed his master of his wife's sin. The labourer repeatedly ran to the priest's home under the guise of carrying out his master's instructions. Each time, he disrupted the lovers – beating the Gypsy under various pretexts – and then brought the priest to witness the affair.

The Gypsy howled like a wolf [hence the title *'vovkulaka'*, cf. werewolf], but he was soon killed, along with the unfaithful wife.

_^_

Comments: This folk tale can be compared to Kolberg's '1.66. The Mistress and the Deacon' on page 79. A similar Ukrainian version appears in Manzhura's collection under the title 'When wolves appeared in the house' (Manzhura 1890, pp. 91–93) and a Polish version can be found in *Lud*, (Kolberg 1857–90, vol. 3, p. 169–172, no. 30).

'Znakhar' by Taras Shevchenko (1842).

1.37. Tymko the Thief and the Chorty

Tymko stole some belongings from a Jew. The Jew promised to gift him the stolen goods if he could steal four oxen harnessed to a plough in broad daylight. Tymko succeeded. He then went on to steal a horse from the stable, a chest full of money, and a maiden, whom he sold to the senior *chort*. Tymko outwitted the *chorty* by defeating them in horseback riding, in a fight with a bear, and in a race with a hare. He eventually reclaimed the maiden and received a reward from the Jew.

_^_

Comments: The tale combines two primary motifs: (1) the skilful thief and (2) the deceit of the *chorty*. Versions of this folk tale can be traced back to the ancient Egyptian legend about the treasure of Rhampsinit, as retold by Herodotus. A brief study on these legends was conducted by Schiefner (1869)[11].

11. Incomplete or incorrect citation in the original.

Further materials on this subject are presented in:

Cosquin (1886, vol. 2, pp. 271–281, no. 70;
Ciszewski (1894, pp. 252–254, no. 202; pp. 267–268, no. 215 – 'Klymko the Thief');
Chelchowski (1890–91, vol. 1, pp. 112–118, no. 17);
Veselovskiy (1882);
Granstrem (1881, pp. 218–219 – the theft of the Sampo);
Sadovnikov (1884, pp. 139–143, no. 31);
Kazbek (1890, p. 83);
Lopatinskiy (1891, p. 130);
Semenov (1893b, p. 103);
Kikot (1893, p. 184);
Maksimilyanov (1893, p. 193);
Lominadze (1894, pp. 27 & 34);
K. G. (1887, p. 343);

Detail of: illustration for Lesia Ukrainka's Lisova Pisnia *[Forest Song] (1911); featuring* chort, *by Olena Sakhnovska (1929).*

Ulanowska (1884, p. 310);
Luzel (1881 vol. 3, p. 367);
Romanov (1887, pp. 410–413, no. 19);
Afanasiev (1873 [?]); and
Pypin (1857, p. 258)[12].

12. Incomplete or incorrect citation in the original.

'The Defence of the Sampo' by Akseli Gallen-Kallela (1896).

1.38. The Magic Bulls of the Angel

A man [poor Ivan] would regularly beat his wife. Each time, she would respond, 'May our Lord, God repay you on my behalf.'

Seeking his 'payment', the man went to heaven, where an Angel gave him a pair of magic bulls. In a single day, the bulls ploughed and levelled an enormous field. Later, they caused the death of Ivan's rich brother by rolling his cart down a hill, sending him to heaven. Ivan then took possession of his brother's estate.

_^_

Comments: The moral of this folk tale is unusual – here, the husband appears to be rewarded for beating his wife. However, the prevailing motif seems to be the luck of the poor brother.

Kolberg included similar Polish folk tales in his *Lud* (1857–90, vol. 14, pp. 233–236, no. 55; & vol. 17, p. 199, no. 12).

Overall, this is one of the crudest folk tales and is likely a distorted version of another, more refined tale.

'Oxen on the ploughing field' (1891) by Serhii Svitoslavskyi.

1.39. The Judgment of God

A robber killed a man in the forest. No one witnessed the crime, but God in heaven told the robber that he would be punished in thirty years. The robber went on to live a prosperous life in his village.

Thirty years later, as the robber was returning from the market with a sack of cabbages over his shoulder, passers-by noticed a human head in his sack instead of a cabbage.

The robber was condemned to the gallows, and his estate was given to the children of the man he had murdered.

_^_

Comments: Morally, this folk tale stands in stark contrast to the preceding one. The theme that fate eventually exposes the villain is widespread across cultures. Similar ideas appear in Friedrich Schiller's ballad 'Die Kraniche des Ibycus' ['The Cranes of Ibycus'] and Hryhoriy Kvitka-Osnovyanenko's story 'Perekatypole' ['Tumbleweed']. I have discussed this theme further in my article 'H. Kvitka as ethnographer' (Sumtsov 1893a).

'Die Kraniche des Ibykus', (1859–1862), by Josef Albert, albumen silver print, housed in the J. Paul Getty Museum, Los Angeles.

1.40. Two Brothers

13. Incomplete or incorrect citation in the original.

When the poor brother found his *Bida* [Misfortune], he trapped it in a jug, buried the jug in a swamp, and soon became rich. The rich brother, believing that the poor brother had discovered treasure in the swamp, unearthed the jug. The *Bida* leapt onto his shoulders, and he lost his fortune.

_^_

Comments: This folk tale exists in many variations. Polish versions can be found in Kolberg's *Lud*, (1857–90, vol. 14, pp. 280–287, no. 70; & vol. 15, p. 10).

Other Ukrainian tales featuring *Zlydni* (a motif similar to *Bida*) include:

Chubynsky (1872–78, vol. 2, pp. 393–400, nos. 110–112: 'About Zlydni', 'Zlydni');
Yastrebov (1894, pp. 78–79 ['Zlydni'];
Wojcieki (1876, pp. 27–33; 'Nędza z Biedą' (Poverty and *Zlydni* / *Bida*); and
Manzhura (1890, pp. 59–60).

Similar folk tales are found among:

Poles (*Wisla* 1890, p. 101)[13];
Georgians (Mashurko 1894, pp. 362, 371 & 372);
the French, and others.

Pavlo Chubynsky (1839–1884), Ukrainian ethnographer and folklorist, best known for his extensive collection of Ukrainian folk tales and songs, published in the multi-volume Works of the Ethnographic and Statistical Expedition *(1872–1878).*

1.41. The Angel in Service on Earth

This legend from Pokuttia tells of an Angel who sinned (the nature of the sin is unspecified) and was exiled to Earth for a year. The Angel became a peasant's labourer, working diligently but never smiling.

One day, the peasant took his labourer to the market. Along the way, the Angel threw stones at a church, bowed to a tavern, and laughed at two potters fighting with their pots. When questioned, he explained to the peasant that a demon was sitting on the church roof, stretching a piece of oxhide to mark people who were chatting or napping during the service. And at the tavern, peasants were discussing the purchase of an icon of Saint Nicholas, and the Angel laughed because he saw that 'earth' was fighting 'earth' for the earth.

Having explained himself, the Angel flew away.

_^_

Comments:

Kolberg's ending to this folk tale is particularly poetic. This legend is familiar to Russian and other cultures, including a well-known version retold by Count Leo Tolstoy as 'What People Live By' (1885).

M. Drahomanov's published an extensive study on this legend in the Bulgarian *Collection of Folk Tales* (1892, pp. 265–291). However, his article omits Kolberg's versions: the Ukrainian variant from Halychyna, published in *Pokucie* (1882–89, vol. 3, pp. 82, 86; vol. 4, p. 200), and the Polish version in *Lud* (Kolberg, 1857–90, vol. 8, p. 165, no. 68).

In 1891, the religious journal *Strannik* published Ponomarev's article[14] discussing folk versions of Tolstoy's story. However, the article is tendentious and polemical, with no relevance to ethnography or literary history.[15]

14. Incomplete or incorrect citation in the original.

15. Other Ukrainian versions of the legend were submitted by M. K. Vasiliev for publication in the *Ethnographical Review* (editor's note in the original: Sumtsov 1894d, p. 111).

1.42. About the Priest, who Slept in Heaven for Three Hundred Years

There was once a very pious and hospitable priest who offered food to poor travellers every day. One day, his brother stole some meat from him and hid it in his bosom, but the meat became stuck to his body. When the brother's wife tried to bite it off, her mouth became stuck to the meat as well.

The Lord, who had dined with the priest, invited him to visit Heaven. There, the priest saw the souls of misers, who appeared as skinny sheep standing on lush grass but unable to graze. He also saw the souls of good people, who, in the form of fat sheep, were grazing even on bare rocks.

After sleeping in Heaven for 300 years, the priest returned to Earth and found a page from the Gospel that had once belonged to him. He then resumed conducting church services.

_–^–_

'Saint Ambrose' (Maliarenko c. 1750s).

Comments: Kolberg recorded a similar Polish folk tale in *Lud* (1857–90, vol. 14, pp. 166–167, no. 36).

This folk tale incorporates three primary motifs:

(1) Sticking or adhesion – previously discussed in the comments on '1.34. How the Young Man Made the Rich Maiden Laugh' on page 53.

(2) The afterlife – drawn from popular eschatological legends. For further analysis, see the works of Veselovskiy (1888) and Shepelevich (1891–92).

(3) The miraculous dream – for more details on this motif, refer to my article 'Sketches on A. Pushkin' (Sumtsov 1893c, part 2).

1.43. Saint Nicholas and his Shepherds

Three sons of a poor man took turns serving as shepherds for Saint Nicholas. The two elder sons received their wages and left, but the youngest son told [Saint Nicholas] that he had been carried to strange, unknown places on the back of a ram. Saint Nicholas explained that the young shepherd had visited hell and witnessed the punishment of misers. As a reward, Saint Nicholas gave him sheep pellets, which magically transformed into gold coins.

_^_

Comments: Kolberg included similar Polish folk tales in *Lud* (1857–90, vol. 3, p. 149, no. 17; & vol. 8, pp. 127–129, no. 51).

(1) The motif of encounters with saintly figures, angels, or God, as seen here and in the previous tale ['1.42. About the Priest, who Slept in Heaven for Three Hundred Years' on page 62], is eschatological in nature.

(2) The transformation motif – the change of sheep pellets into gold coins – represents a variation of the widespread motif of coal transforming into gold. For further details, see my review of Romanov's *Belarusian Collection* (Sumtsov 1894e).

Icon of Saint Nicholas from Oster town, Chernihiv region, Ukraine (17th century).

Icon of Saint Nicholas from Chorniyiv village, Volyn region, Ukraine (17th century).

1.44. Three Pieces of Advice

A labourer agreed to serve for three years in exchange for three pieces of advice: (1) Do not enter the water if you don't know the ford. (2) Do not lend your cattle. (3) Do not let your wife go out to make merry on her own.

The labourer later saw a hussar drowning and took his horse and clothing. Ignoring the second piece of advice, he lent his horse to a priest, and the horse gave birth to a foal while under a heavy load. Disregarding the third piece of advice, he allowed his wife to attend a wedding. Disguised as a hussar, the labourer went to the wedding himself. There, his wife became enamoured with the 'hussar' and agreed to sleep with him for five gold coins, with her mother's approval. In the end, the labourer killed both his wife and his mother-in-law for their deeds.

_^_

Comments: The motif of acquiring two or three pieces of advice has immense literary significance due to its widespread presence in the Old World. It appears in *Ruodlieb*, an 11th-century Latin novel, as well as in fables from the 12th and 13th centuries and in the folk tales of many contemporary peoples. This motif is likely of East Asian origin. I will not discuss it in detail here, as I am preparing a monograph on the subject for publication.

1.45. Adventures of the Foundling

A foundling met a woman, married her without knowing she was his mother, and had a carnal relationship with her. When he discovered her true identity, he locked himself in a house by the sea and threw the key into the water.

Twenty years later, during the election of a Pope, it was decided that the one whose candle lit by itself would be chosen. The hermit's candle miraculously lit up, and he became the Pope.

_^_

Comments: This folk tale blends two well-known and widely distributed motifs:

(1) The motif of incest with one's own mother, a theme extensively developed in songs.

(2) The motif of the repentant sinner, previously discussed in, '1.7. The Power of Repentance' on page 31.

Ukrainian songs featuring the first motif can be found in:
Chubynsky (1872–78, vol. 5, p. 201, no. 407);
Holovatsky (1878, vol. 1 pp. 45, 75 & vol. 2, p. 577);
Antonovych & Drahomanov 1874-75, vol. 1, p. 275);
Kolberg (1882–89, vol. 2, pp. 29 & 35);
Nejman (1884c, pp. 115–246); and
Shein (1874, p. 143)[16].

16. Incomplete or incorrect citation in the original.

НЕСЧАСТНАЯ ЛЮБОВЬ.

407.

У Полтаві на риночку
Пьють козаки горілочку;
Пили жъ вони, гуляли,
На шинкарку гукали:
— Шинкарочка молода,
Повірь меду й вина.—
„Не повірю, не продамъ,
„Бо на тобі жупанъ дранъ"
— Хочь на мині жупанъ дранъ—
Єсть у мене грошей джбанъ.—
„Якъ у тебе грошей джбанъ,
Я за тебе дочку дамъ;
А дочку, не наймичку,
Присталую панночку.
Якъ вона заговорить,
Мовъ у дзвони задзвонить;
Якъ вона засміється—
Мовъ Дунай розіллється!"
У суботу змовлялись,
А въ неділю звінчались,
А зъ вінчання вертались,
Свого роду питались:
— Скажи мині, серденько,

— Якого ти родоньку?
„Я зъ Кієва Петрівна,
По батькові Йванівна."
Скажи мині, серденько,
Я кого ти родоньку?"
Я зъ Кієва Петренко,
По батькові Йваненко!
Який теперъ світъ настав,
Що братъ сестри не пізнавъ!
— Ходімъ, сестро, горою,
Розсіємось травою;
Ходімъ, сестро, степами;
Розсіємось цвітами!
Ой ти будешъ жовтий цвітъ,
А я буду синій цвітъ!
Будуть люде косити —
За насъ Бога моліти;
Будуть люде цвіти рвати —
Изъ насъ гріхи збірати.
Стануть люде казати:
Отсе жъ тая—травиця:
Що въ братікомъ сестриця!

(Изъ Рук. Сборн. Н. И. Костомарова).

Song 'Unhappy Love' (Chubynsky, 1872–78, vol. 5, p. 201, no. 407).

'Rus peasants from Chortkiv county, eastern Halychyna', (Holovatsky 1878, vol. 3, p. 263).

1.46. Punished Greed

Three brothers inherited their father's estate, but the youngest brother did not receive his share. Despite this, he became wealthy on his own. Curious about the source of his wealth, the older brothers questioned him. The youngest brother tricked them by selling them a wolf, claiming it was a talisman for breeding sheep. The wolf, however, strangled all their sheep.

He then told them that money fell from his wife's *namitka* when he struck her on the head with a club. Believing him, the older brothers killed their wives and had to flee.

_^_

Comments: This tale belongs to the extensive tradition of stories about the cunning deceiver:

'A village woman' (end 18th century), illustration by Kalynskyi Tymofiy, featuring a woman wearing namitka.

Yastrebov (1894, pp. 129–130, no. 6);

Drahomanov (1876, pp. 343–347, no. 28);

Chubynsky (1872–78, vol. 2, pp. 350–353, 514–517 & 503–504);

Rudchenko (1869 –70, vol. 2, pp. 125–136);

Lominadze (1894, p. 30 (a Mingrelian tale);

Chelchowski (1890–91, vol. 1, pp. 76–83, no. 11);

Luzel (1881, vol. 3, pp. 315 & 418); and

Cosquin (1886, vol. 1 pp. 108–119, no. 10, pp. 222–231, & no. 20 & pp. 263–267, no. 26. Cosquin also references numerous other versions, primarily under no. 20 (1886, vol. 1, pp. 222–231).

1.47. The Rich Man and the Poor Man

Two brothers lived: one was wealthy, and the other was poor. The poor brother pretended to be dead and was laid out in the funeral parlour. When robbers entered to divide their loot, he made some noises, startling them. Terrified, they fled, leaving their stolen money behind.

The rich brother, [envious of his brother's success], attempted the same trick. However, the robbers caught him and killed him.

_^_

Comments: A similar version of this folk tale appears below as, '1.57. Three Brothers' on page 74.

The motif of the poor man who scares away robbers and takes their wealth is widely known in folk traditions. For related versions, see:
Cosquin (1886, vol. 1, pp. 108–119, no. 10, pp. 222–231, no. 20 & pp. 237–245, no. 22);
Vereshchagin (1886, p. 160);
Sadovnikov (1884, pp. 126–132, no. 27);
Chelchowski (1890–91, vol. 2, pp. 12–14, no. 49);
K. G. (1887, p. 341); and
Hahn (1864, vol. 2, p. 238).

1.48. Breast Milk as a Remedy for an Eye Ailment

A rich man went blind. With the help of a *chort*, a poor man found a woman who had been a virgin when she married. He asked for her breast milk, used it to cure the rich man's blindness, and received a reward.

_^_

Comments: I am unaware of another folk tale of this kind. However, in the Kharkiv province, I have often heard the folk belief that breast milk, applied directly from the nipple, is the best remedy for eye diseases. This belief likely stems from the observation that mothers use breast milk to wash away eye discharge from their infants' eyes.

1.49. Three Riddles

A *Pan* unknowingly slept with his own daughter, who later gave birth to a child. The doctor, using forceps, delivered a premature but handsome boy. He placed the infant next to his own wife, who had also just given birth, and told her that she had twins.

The boys grew up together, but after quarrelling at school, they went their separate ways. Following his mother's advice, the illegitimate son cut the skin from her breast, made mittens from it, and bought a prematurely born horse.

The hero then posed three riddles to the Tsarivna: "The non-living rides the non-living, wearing mittens made from his mother's skin." Unable to solve the riddles, the Tsarivna had to marry him.

_^_

Comments: A similar Ukrainian version appears in Moszynska's collection (1885, pp. 134–137, no. 25), [here, see '2.25. The Riddle-Tale' on page 138].

Russian versions of this tale were published in Khomiakov's collections (recorded, if I recall correctly, by the well-known writer Kokhapovskaya).

A related Polish folk version was published in *Wisla* (Mo[szk]ow 1891).

1.50 & 1.51. The Wise Maiden

A young man and his *svaty* arrived at a young woman's home while her parents were away and asked if her parents would return soon.

The young woman replied, 'They will return soon if they take the longer route; but it will take a while if they take a shortcut and get lost.'

She then asked whether they had tethered their horse to winter or summer (meaning a sleigh or a wagon), and what to serve them for supper: something that increases (cheese), decreases (*kovbasa*), or falls off the body (egg).[17]

_^_

Comments: Another Ukrainian version of this tale appears in Moszynska's collection 1885, pp. 137–140, no. 26) [here, see '2.26. Hurka, the Seven-Year-Old Girl' on page 139], while a Polish version can be found in Kolberg's *Lud* (1857–90, vol. 14, pp. 265–268, no. 66).

The tale centres on the widely popular motif of the wise maiden, which recurs in various forms across apocrypha, novels, legends, folk tales, and songs. Buslaev analysed an old Russian story about *Peter and Fevronia* in his *Historical Sketches* (Buslaev, 1861). Extensive lists of references are also included in Child's *The English and Scottish Popular Ballads* (Child, 1882–98) and in the supplements to *Wisla* (1889 and 1890).[18]

17. The folk tale unfolds as a series of riddles.

18. Incomplete or incorrect citation in the original.

'The Poor Man, the Rich Man, and the Dark-Haired Girl'. Illustration by Mahalevsky Yuriy (*Rudchenko* 1920d, p. 23).

1.52. The Liar and the Fibber

A liar was walking through the village when the *Pan* saw him and asked, 'How big is the neighbouring *Pan's* harvest?'

The liar replied, 'Our *Pan* grew such a large cabbage that they covered the house roof with just one leaf.'

Later, the *Pan* encountered an even greater liar. When asked whether it was true that a cabbage leaf had been used to cover the roof, this liar claimed, 'I saw them dragging that cabbage to be used instead of a wooden block in the mill.'

The *Pan* then met yet another liar, who told him, 'The neighbouring *Pan* had such tall buckwheat that he got lost in the field while hunting and couldn't find his way out for three days.'

Finally, the *Pan* spoke to [the greatest] fibber of all. This one added, 'I saw Gypsies uprooting the buckwheat stumps to use as firewood.'

_^_

Hryhoriy Kvitka-Osnovyanenko (1778–1843), a Ukrainian writer and civic leader, is renowned for his prose works.

Comments: On this topic, Hryhoriy Kvitka-Osnovyanenko wrote a comic novella 'Pidbrekhach' ['A Fibber'], which I analyse in my article, 'H. Kvitka as Ethnographer' (Sumtsov 1893a).

Pokotyhoroshko flying on an eagle (Lukashevych, 1909, p. 30)

1.53. About the Deaf Village

Everyone in the village was deaf, which led to a series of misunderstandings. A peasant was searching for his lost goats, but a deaf man thought he was being scolded for putting up a fence in his yard. The peasant gifted him a hornless goat, but the deaf man believed he was being accused of mutilating the goat, and so on.

_^_

Comments: Folk anecdotes about deafness are widespread (e. g. Yastrebov 1894, p. 181, no. 37)

Pushkin also knew a version of this anecdote, which inspired his poem, 'The deaf was calling the deaf' [1830].

1.54. The Foolish Son

The foolish son complained to his father that a Gypsy had struck him on one side of his face, twisting it, and then hit him on the other side to straighten it. Misunderstanding his father's words, the son ended up calling his father a simpleton.

1.55. The Swindler against the Swindler

Ivan the Servant tricked the *Pan* into spending the night in the forest, while he himself dined with the gentry, flying from an oak tree.

1.56. About the Foolish Hutsul Soldier

A Hutsul soldier stood guard while chatting with his wife and eating *varenyky*.

Suddenly, the Major appeared and asked how long he had been in the service.

The Hutsul said, 'Guess.'

The Major said, 'A year.'

The Hutsul said, 'Lower.'

The Major kept lowering the number, and the Hutsul repeated 'Lower,' until the former reached 'Nine weeks.'

Then the Hutsul asked, 'What [rank] are you?'

The Major offered to let him guess.

The Hutsul began with 'Corporal.'

The Major said, 'Higher.'

This continued until the Hutsul finally reached 'Major.'

_^_

Comments: This anecdote is widely known. I have also heard it in connection with Emperor, Joseph II of Austria and his gardener.

1.57. Three Brothers

There were three brothers: two were clever, and the third was foolish. The foolish brother ignored all the advice of his older brothers. He killed their mother, destroyed the funeral items, and while hiding with his brothers from robbers in the forest atop an oak tree, he defecated on the robbers' heads and dropped their mother's bed. The robbers fled in terror.

_^_

Comments: Kolberg references a Greek version of this folk tale, entitled 'Bakala' and contained in Hahn's collection (1864, vol. 2, p. 238; Kolberg 1882-89, vol. 4, p. 235). For additional versions of this tale, see '1.47. The Rich Man and the Poor Man' on page 69.

1.58. Three Sons

While in the forest, a father asked his three sons what could be made from oak. From their answers, he realised that his two older sons would become good masters, while the youngest would turn into a robber. The youngest son then deceived his father and stole a ram from him.

_^_

Comments: Kolberg included a similar Polish folk tale in *Lud* (1857–90), vol. 8, pp. 107–114 no. 43).

'Hutsuls in Forest' (c. 1872) by Artur Grottger (1837–1867).

1.59. The Fortunate Purchase

A poor man sold his last cow and used the money to buy a foundling [a boy] at the market. The boy then stole oxen from the field, as well as a *Pan's* possessions and other items, thereby enriching his master.

_^_

Comments: This tale is a version of '1.37. Tymko the Thief and the Chorty' on page 56. In this version, the thief is called Klymko. Polish versions of similar folk tales are included in *Lud* (Kolberg 1857–90, vol. 14, pp. 291–292, no. 73; and vol. 19, p. 243, no. 19).

1.60. The Fortunate Sale

Two brothers sold their oxen at the fair, but the third brother sold his ox to an aspen tree. When the tree creaked, the foolish brother thought it was talking to him. That night, wolves ate the ox. Believing the aspen tree had 'eaten' his ox and failed to pay for it, the foolish brother began chopping it down. To his surprise, money fell from the tree, and he ended up receiving far more than his clever brothers.

'Working Behind the Plough', Zhivopisnaya Rossiya, *1897, vol. 5, p. 14.*

Comments: Polish versions of this folk tale are included in *Lud* (Kolberg 1857–90, vol. 8, pp. 201–202, no. 81; and vol. 17, p. 199, no. 12.)

A Russian version featuring a simpleton and a birch tree is also well known.

1.61. The Cunning Shoemaker

The cunning shoemaker, unwilling to work, acquired bread, *horilka*, and money through deceit, putting it all on the credit of a rich woman and a priest – without their knowledge.

_^_

Comments: This is a rough folk tale of recent origin, reflecting an unambiguous approval of theft.

1.62. The Thief in Confession

Soldier the Thief stole some pork from the priest's bowl of *borshch*, wolf fur, and a hat that was lying in front of the icons. During his confession, he claimed that he had driven the pig out of the garden, chased the wolf away, and removed a hat in reverence before the icons.[19] He was praised for his actions. However, during the confession, Soldier the Thief also managed to steal four rubles from the priest.

_^_

Comments: A similar Ukrainian folk tale is found in Ivan Manzhura's collection (1890, p. 110);

Belarusian: Dobrovolskiy (1891, pp. 700–701, no. 13);

Russian: Afanasiev (1873 [?]);

Kryptadia, vol. 1, p. 50; and

Corsican – in Ortoli (1883, pp. 19–24, no. 4 'L'anneau De la Princesse').

19. In Ukraine, it is customary to remove one's hat in front of icons, in church, or indoors in general.

1.63. The Theft of the Cloak (Priest's Garment)

A thief claimed he wanted to buy a cloak for his brother and asked the salesman to try it on. When the salesman removed his clothes, the thief stole them. Left wearing only the cloak, the victim ran after the thief, but other merchants mistook him for the thief.

1.64. The Theft of the Kozhukh

A soldier saw an old woman wearing a new *kozhukh* and told her she reminded him of his mother. He began to ply her with *horilka*. The old woman, excited, took off her *kozhukh* and started to dance. At that moment, the soldier stole her *kozhukh*.

_^_

Comments: A similar Belarusian version is found in Romanov 1887, p. 427, no. 28, and a Polish version in Kolberg's collections (1857, p. 281 and *Lud*, 1857–90, vol. 19, p. 247, no. 22). [...]

1.65. The Husband and Three Lovers of his Wife

The miller, the priest, and the head of the village all arrived to visit a woman at the same time. She sent each of them onto the *pich* to hide. When her husband returned, he kept them on the hot *pich* for a long time. Then, pretending to set the house on fire, he forced the lovers to flee naked.

_^_

Comments: Folk tales and stories on this topic are discussed in articles by M. Sumtsov (1892) and M. Dashkevych (1893).

'I don't know what other food to offer you, Afanasiy Ivanovych!' by V. Makovsky (1885); illustration for M. Hohol's comedy 'The Fair at Sorochyntsi' (1875); featuring Khyvria, a married woman, and A. I., the son of the village priest, during their secret rendezvous. A. I. is holding a varenyk *on his fork.*

1.66. The Mistress and the Deacon

A man's wife was having an affair with the deacon. The husband's labourer decided to punish the lovers. By substituting their oxen, he tricked the wife into going to the field where her husband was working instead of meeting the deacon. The labourer then warned the deacon that the husband was planning to kill him and told the husband that the deacon had asked him to repair his cart. When the deacon saw the husband approaching with an axe, he fled in fear, and the wife confessed her infidelity to her husband.

_^_

Comments: This folk tale is a version of '1.36. The Unfaithful Wife and the Vovkulaka' on page 55. Another similar Ukrainian version appears in Ivan Manzhura's collection (1890, pp. 91–93).

Polish versions are found in Kolberg's *Lud* (1857–90, vol. 3, p. 168, nos. 29 & 30; vol. 14, pp. 335–337, no. 95; vol. 21, pp. 193–197, no. 12).

1.67. The Deacon and the Unfaithful Wife

The husband pretended to be deaf and blind. When his wife was offering *varenyky* to the church deacon, the husband killed him and stuck a *varenyk* into his mouth. The wife thought that the deacon choked [on her *varenyky*].

The husband carried the corpse to the priest's apiary. The priest fired a shot, and [when he saw the dead deacon] he thought that he killed a thief. He paid the husband, as the only witness, to keep silent.

The husband then placed the corpse on the *Pan's* threshing floor. The *Pan* also fired a shot and paid the husband for his silence.

_^_

Comments: For a version of this folk tale, see '1.69. The Old Woman, who was Buried Four Times' on page 81, where I list references on the subject.

1.68. Adventures of the Child

Illustration for 'The Man, the Wolf, the Boar, and the Bear' (Lukashevych, 1909, p. 59).

This folk tale tells of a child whose evil aunt gave him away to the Gypsies. The Gypsies taught him to steal horses, but when one of them attempted to kill him, the boy fled and joined a group of comedians. When the Gypsy later tried to strangle him, a bear saved the boy.

_^_

Comments: This tale represents a newer variation of folk tales about the abduction of children by Gypsies.

1.69. The Old Woman, who was Buried Four Times

_^_

Comments: This tale is a variation of '1.67. The Deacon and the Unfaithful Wife' on page 80.

Folk tales featuring the movement of a corpse from place to place are widespread across many cultures. In earlier times, this motif also appeared in novels, fables, and short stories. The fable 'Le sacristain de Cluny' with a similar theme was published in the renowned collections of E. Barbazan, and M. Meon, and Montagnion[20]. One of Boccaccio stories also aligns with this motif.

Ukrainian folk tales on this topic were published in:

Yastrebov (1894, p. 169, no. 29);

Ulanowska (1884 p. 311);

Manzhura (1890, p. 76–77);

Russian:

Afanasiev (1873 [?]);

Sadovnikov (1884, pp. 162–163, no. 42);

Kryptadia, (vol. 1, pp. 240-245, no. 68);

Polish: Chelchowski (1890–91, vol. 1, pp. 54–62, no. 7 & pp. 88–95, no. 14);

Serbian: *Vrana*[21];

The Caucasus:

Nasir-Sultanov (1892, p. 306);

Riabykh (1893, p. 301);

Votyak (Udmurt) folk tale:

Vereshchagin (1886, p. 163);

French and other *Western [European]*: Cosquin (1886, vol. 2, pp. 333–337, no. 80); and

Indian: Minaev (1876, p. 89).

20. Incomplete or incorrect citation in the original – the name of the author is probably misspelt.

21. Incomplete or incorrect citation in the original.

1.70. About the Old Man's Goats

The old man (described as evil, with a grey beard, red boots, and a gold mace) sent his son to herd his goats. The goats ate well, but upon returning home, they claimed to be hungry. [As punishment], the Old Man killed his son. The same happened when he sent his daughter and then his wife – each time, the goats lied, and the old man killed his wife and daughter.

Finally, the old man decided to herd the goats himself. The goats lied to him as well. In anger, he began flaying them. One half-flayed goat escaped and hid under the *pich*, scaring everyone by singing, "I'm a flayed goat..." Only a crayfish confronted it, saying, "I'm Crayfish the Brave; if I pinch you, there'll be a mark!" And drove the goat out from under the *pich*.

_^_

22. Incomplete or incorrect citation in the original.

Comments: Folk tales about deceitful goats are widespread and appear in many cultures with similar plots. Analogous Ukrainian versions were published in:

Chubynsky (1872–78, vol. 2, p. 128);

Moszynska (1885, pp. 111–113, no. 11; here, see '2.11. The Old Man's Goats' on page 120);

23. Incomplete or incorrect citation in the original.

Russian:

Afanasiev (1873 [?]);

Sadovnikov (1884, pp. 179-183, no. 55);

Polish:

Ulanowska (1884, p. 308);[22]

> „Ja koza-dereza, piv boka obderta,
> koho jmu, toho wbju,
> a rohamy nakujn,
> pid picz fostom zametu".

(Kolberg 1882–89, vol. 4, p. 263).

> „A ja rak nyborak,
> de uszcziepnu bude znak".

(Kolberg 1882–89, vol. 4, p. 265).

Karlowicz (1888, p. 42, no. 76, 'Gadająca koza');
Chelchowski (1890–91, vol. 1, pp. 180–183, no. 28); and
Wisla 1890, p. 77[23].

Serbian: Karadžić (1870, pp. 244–246, no. 13);

French and other Western [European] folk tales in: Cosquin (1886, vol. 2, pp. 115–117, no. 47).

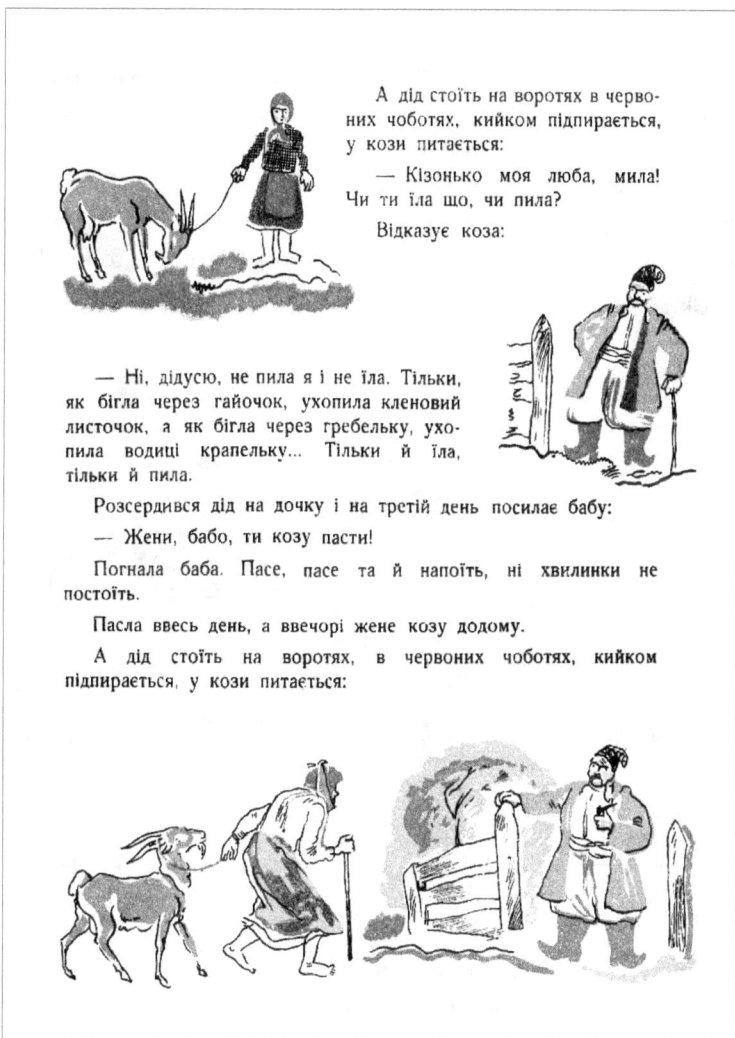

А дід стоїть на воротях в червоних чоботях, кийком підпирається, у кози питається:

— Кізонько моя люба, мила! Чи ти їла що, чи пила?

Відказує коза:

— Ні, дідусю, не пила я і не їла. Тільки, як бігла через гайочок, ухопила кленовий листочок, а як бігла через гребельку, ухопила водиці крапельку... Тільки й їла, тільки й пила.

Розсердився дід на дочку і на третій день посилає бабу:

— Жени, бабо, ти козу пасти!

Погнала баба. Пасе, пасе та й напоїть, ні хвилинки не постоїть.

Пасла ввесь день, а ввечорі жене козу додому.

А дід стоїть на воротях, в червоних чоботях, кийком підпирається, у кози питається:

Illustrations by Borys Kriukov for Koza-Dereza folk tale (Kriukov 1929, p. 4).

1.71. The Dog and the Wolf

The Wolf ordered boots from the Hungry Dog. In payment, the Dog demanded horse meat and ate it. Next, he demanded *salo* and ate that too. Finally, the Dog lured the Wolf to his former owner's pantry, where he made the Wolf drunk. When the Wolf began to sing (howl), he was killed

_^_

Comments: The second half of the tale often appears as a separate story. The conflict between the wolf and the dog is a recurring theme. Typically, a bear and a wild boar side with the wolf, while a cat, duck, and goose support the dog. The cat ultimately overcomes and scatters the wolf's allies.

This is a version of the famous Ukrainian folk tale about a dog named Sirko.

A Polish version of the folk tale can be found in Kolberg's *Lud* (1857–90, vol. 14, p. 327, no. 89).

Illustration by Petro Lapyn, for Sirko *fork tale, (Todosiv 1920).*

1.72. The Donkey, the Bear and the Wolf

The Donkey and the Bear quarrelled and went their separate ways. The Wolf sided with the Bear and planned to tear the Donkey apart. However, as the Bear had tied himself to the Wolf's tail, he [accidentally] tore the Wolf's tail off along the way, causing the Wolf to die.

'Madey' (Wojcieki 1876, p. 104).

1.73. Koshalky–Opalky

_^_

Comments: This Hutsul folk tale closely resembles another Ukrainian folk tale in the collection of J. Moszynska (Moszynska 1885, pp. 146–148, no. 29) [see '2.29. About the Wise Simpleton' on page 144].

The unusual title of the Hutsul folk tale, 'Koshalky-opalky', meaning a tall tale, is not commonly known in Ukraine. Kolberg's version of the folk tale is notably longer than J. Moszynska's version.

The plot is conventional: the hero, a simpleton, tells an exaggerated tall tale to a monstrous old man and, according to their agreement, removes a strip of his skin.

For relevant references, see my comments on J. Moszynska's folk tale, '2.29. About the Wise Simpleton' on page 144.

'Hutsuls' by Leon Zienkowicz (1841).

'Koshalky-Opalky' (Wojcieki 1876, p. 145).

1.74. The Fairy Tale about the Diamond Road

_^_

Comments: This is a version of the Ukrainian folk tale about *Pokoty-horoshko*[24], widely known from collections by Chubynsky (1872–78, vol. 2, pp. 229–231, 231–236 & 236–239) and Moszynska (1885, pp. 97–99) [here, see '2.7. Pokotyhoroshko' on page 113], etc. This Hutsul folk tale stands out due to its distinctive ending – a song, which is rarely found in folk tales:

> 'The emperor held a big gathering on that occasion,
> Everyone was drinking and dancing.
> I was there too,
> And I observed all kind of beauty.
> At the end I became bored,
> Something bothered me,
> I would rather return home,
> No more folk tales to tell.
> Let everyone think what they want,
> The Hutsul is telling the truth about
> How it used to be in the world,
> Now everything that was good has passed [...]'

24. Pokotyhoroshko –
Also 'Kotyhoroshko';
'Roll-A-Pea'

1.75. About the Lazy Son

[The Old Woman had] a son so lazy that he refused to fetch even water. One day, he accidentally caught the Golden Fish, which begged him to let her go. As a reward, the Golden Fish made his *pich* fetch water by itself.

Later, the Tsarivna ate a golden apple and miraculously became pregnant. Her father exiled her, and she wandered the world with the hero of this tale. The Tsarivna had a golden handkerchief, which she exchanged for a magic table that provided food. She then traded the table for a stick-samobiy (self-beating stick) and used the stick to acquire a magic wand. With the wand, they built a magnificent palace.

_^_

Comments: This folk tale combines two motifs:

(1) A motif of the Golden Fish helping the hero, which I intend to analyse in depth in my 'Sketches on A. Pushkin' (cf. Sumtsov 1893c),

particularly in relation to [Pushkin's] verse tale about the Golden Fish;[25] and

(2) The motif of miraculous conception, which appears across folklore worldwide. Folk tales involving miraculous conceptions are numerous and deserve a separate study.

25. M. Sumtsov refers to Pushkin's 'The tale of the fisherman and the fish' (1835).

Key references include:

Cosquin (1886, vol. 1, pp. 1–27, no. 1, pp. 60–81, no. 5, pp. 120–132, no. 11 & vol. 2, pp. 164–167, no. 55; conception via wheat, apple, water, fish, or dragon's heart);

Manzhura (1890, pp. 24–27 (fish), pp. 28–30 (fish, eel) & pp. 30–33 (peas);

Minaev (1876, pp. 114–118; fruit);

Kolberg, (1882–89, vol. 4, p. 34; heart);

Maspero (1889, p. 30; a wood chip);

Granstrem (1881, p. 234; berry – Marjatta became pregnant from a lingonberry);

Kolberg (1857–90, vol. 8, no. 63; caviar);

Karadžić (1870, pp. 103–105, no. 24; snow);

Sadovnikov (1884, pp. 103–104, no. 20 (snow) & pp. 133–134, no. 28 (apple);

Khudiakov (1860–62, vol. 2, pp. 43–46, no. 46; fish);

Potanin (1881–83, issue 2, p. 162; water);

Kikot (1893, p. 189);

Lopatinskiy (1891; an apple);

Dobrovolskiy (1891, p. 624; a pea);

The Völsunga Saga (an apple);

Hahn (1864, vol. 1, no. 21 (laurel) & no. 54 (peas) & vol. 2, no. 99 (nuts), vol. 1, nos. 6 & 22 and vol. 2, no. 68; (apples);

Potebnia (1881, p. 76);

Luzel (1881, vol. 1, pp. 45 & 60; a thought); and

Ovid's The Metamorphoses (the rain of gold).

This motif can be traced back to ancient tales, facetiae, and jokes, which later served as the foundation for modern fables, such as Aleksandr Izmaylov's fable The Snow Child. Among Russian scholars, only academic A. Veselovskiy (1880) provided a thorough analysis of miraculous conception motifs, notably in his reviews of Chubynsky's Works (1872–78) and the Romanian folk tale collection by Kremnitz (1882).

A [Belarusian] folk tale (Romanov 1887, no. 8, pp. 67–73) tells of Ivan Zlatovus [cf. John Chrysostom], whose mother was impregnated by a whirlwind. Similar motifs appear in other Belarusian tales in Romanov's *Belarusian Collection* (1887, vol. 3, nos. 13, 15, pp. 92–99, 110–120). In another version, Pokotyhoroshko's mother conceives him after eating three peas.

In the folklore of various peoples, virgins become pregnant by eating a fish, apple, or other round fruit, or by swallowing a snowflake, hailstone, or merely touching a stone.

Mongolian folk tales claim human ancestors emerged from a bear, swan, birch, tree stump, saliva, or hailstone (Potanin 1881–83, issue 2, pp. 161–163, no. 19). In Caucasian folklore, conception often results from eating an apple (Teptsov 1894, pp. 17 & 23 and Eivazov 1894, p. 85). In Ukrainian folklore, peas play a central role (Kolberg 1882–89, vol. 4, pp. 280–286, no. 74; Moszynska 1885, pp. 97–99, no. 7; see '2.7. Pokotyhoroshko' on page 113.

'Danae and the Shower of Gold' by Peter Paul Rubens (undated).

1.76. A Fairy Tale about a Clever Furrier

The Tsar asked the furrier how he managed to survive on his earnings. The Furrier replied that he earned eight coins a day: he lent out two coins, repaid a debt with two, wasted two, and lived on the remaining two.

Puzzled, the Tsar ordered his ministers to solve the riddle. The ministers gave the Furrier money in hopes of receiving an answer, but he refused to explain it to them.

Finally, the furrier explained to the Tsar that two coins were spent on raising his son, two on supporting his parents, two on his daughter and son-in-law, and the last two on himself and his wife.

_^_

Comments: In this tale, the Furrier assumes the role of the Wise Maiden, making this a variation of the folk tales listed under 1.50 & 1.51 with references to the literature on the subject, see p. 70.

'The old woman' (Lukashevych, 1909, p. 143)

1.77. About Tsarivna Nesmiyana

On Easter Day, a dog ate a blessed piglet. The owner, seeking justice, complained to the village chief, then to the mandator (policeman), and so on, until he finally reached the Tsar. Upon hearing the peasant's long and absurd tale of his journey through the ranks, the Tsar's daughter, who had been quiet and sad, burst into laughter.

_^_

Comments: This is a variation of the folk tale '1.34. How the Young Man Made the Rich Maiden Laugh' on page 53.

List of leading motifs in Kolberg's folk tales

The list is derived from Mykola Sumtsov's compilation of motifs found in folk tales collected by Kolberg (Sumtsov 1894b, pp. 120–121). Entries marked with an asterisk (*) are retained from Sumtsov's original work, while the remaining entries are new additions derived from the author's commentaries.

Motif	Folk tale no.
Impossible tasks*	no. 1.1.
Miraculous transformation of lovers	no. 1.1.
Impossible tasks*	no. 1.2.
Baba Yaga (Yazia-Zmiya)	no. 1.2.
Tsarivna who speaks, and gold flows from her lips	no. 1.2.
Magic objects*	no. 1.2.
Mare's Head	no. 1.3.
Magic objects*	no. 1.4.
Marko the Rich	nos. 1.5. & 1.6.
Parricide	no. 1.7.
The repentance of the sinner (robber)*	no. 1.7.
Parricide*	no. 1.7.
Child substitution*	no. 1.8.

Motif	Folk tale no.
Wicked (envious) woman*	no. 1.8.
Severed finger	no. 1.9.
Substitution	no. 1.11.
Magic objects*	no. 1.12.
Grateful animals*	nos. 1.13 & 1.14.
Life-giving water	nos. 1.13 & 1.14.
Imposter husband	no. 1.15.
Traitorous mother or wife*	no. 1.16. & 1.17.
Impossible tasks*	no. 1.18.
Helpful giants: *Obpyvalo, Obyidalo**	no. 1.18.
A contest of strength between a bear and a human	no. 1.19.
Squeezing water from a stone or crushing it to prove strength	no. 1.19.
Pinched paws, beards*	no. 1.19.
Sons keeping watch over their father's grave	no. 1.20.
The Glass Mountain	no. 1.20.
The rescue of a *Tsarivna*	no. 1.20.
Impossible tasks*	no. 1.21.
Acquiring a magical bird's feather*	no. 1.21.
The hero arrives at a wedding in disguise as a musician (violinist)	no. 1.21.
The grateful revenant (*mrets*)	no. 1.22.
Magic objects*	no. 1.22.
The repentance of the sinner (robber)*	nos. 1.24.–1.26.
Madey's Bed	no. 1.26.
The repentance of the sinner (robber)*	no. 1.27.
Impossible tasks*	no. 1.28.
Madey's Bed	no. 1.28.
Chort wearing human skin	no. 1.29.
The quest to discover what instils fear*	no. 1.30.

Motif	Folk tale no.
Chort wearing human skin	no. 1.31.
Torments of the bread*	no. 1.32.
Miserly priest	no. 1.33.
A poor young man makes a sad rich maiden laugh	no. 1.34.
Bohatyri of animal origin: the Son of Mare, the Son of Bear (Medvidko)*	no. 1.35.
A cunning labourer	nos. 1.35. & 1.36.
A skilled thief*	no. 1.37.
Magic objects*	no. 1.38.
Divine justice and the inescapable punishment of a hidden crime	no. 1.39.
Zlydni*	no. 1.40.
Repentance of an angel*	no. 1.41.
Transformation of objects into gold	no. 1.43.
Buying advice*	no. 1.44.
Incest with one's mother*	no. 1.45.
The repentance of the sinner (robber)*	no. 1.45.
The cunning deceiver and the unintended killing of wives*	no. 1.46.
A poor man or simpleton outwits robbers and benefits from their abandoned wealth*	no. 1.47.
Breast milk as a remedy for blindness or eye ailments	no. 1.48.
Riddle-solving as a test of wisdom*	no. 1.49.
The wise maiden*	nos. 1.50 & 1.51.
Riddle-solving as a test of wisdom*	nos. 1.50 & 1.51.
Exaggeration and tall tales	no. 1.52.
Misunderstandings leading to humour or conflict	nos. 1.53. & 1.54.
Exaggeration and tall tales	no. 1.55.
Misunderstandings leading to humour or conflict	no. 1.56.

Motif	Folk tale no.
A poor man or simpleton outwits robbers and benefits from their abandoned wealth*	no. 1.57.
Revealing fate through questions	no. 1.58.
A skilled thief*	nos. 1.58. & 1.59.
The foolish brother who gains unexpected wealth	no. 1.60.
A skilled thief*	nos. 1.61.–1.64.
Unfaithful wife*	nos. 1.65.–1.67.
Corpse relocation*	nos. 1.67. & 1.69.
Child abduction and rescue	no. 1.68.
Malevolent livestock (i.e. *Koza-Dereza* or the malicious goat)*	no. 1.70.
Conflict and deception between animals	nos. 1.71.& 1.72.
Exaggeration and tall tales	no. 1.74.
Miraculous conception*	nos. 1.74. & 1.75.
The wise maiden*	no. 1.76.
Riddle-solving as a test of wisdom*	no. 1.76.
A poor young man makes a sad rich maiden laugh	no. 1.77.

Citations of the Folk Tales in Kolberg's Original

'1. Królewicz i czartowska córka' [The king's son and the *chort's* daughter], pp. 3–7 (Kolberg 1882–89, vol. 4), recorded in Spas and Myshyn villages, near Kolomyia town.

'2. Córka i pasierbica' [The daughter and the stepdaughter], pp. 7–14 (Kolberg 1882–89, vol. 4), recorded in Khotymyr village near Obertyn village.

'3. Córka i pasierbica: Odmiana' [The daughter and the stepdaughter: a variant], pp. 14–21 (Kolberg 1882–89, vol. 4), recorded in Spas and Myshyn villages.

'4. Cudowny kamień' [The magic stone], pp. 21–25 (Kolberg 1882–89, vol. 4), recorded in Nezvysko and Herasymiv villages.

'5. Urodzony pod szczęsną gwiazdą' [The one born under a lucky star], pp. 25–31 (Kolberg 1882–89, vol. 4), recorded in Chortovets village.

'6. Posłaniec zięciem' [Son-in-law, the messenger], pp. 31–34 (Kolberg 1882–89, vol. 4), recorded in Spas and Myshyn villages.

'7. Moc pokuty' [The power of repentance], pp. 34–38 (Kolberg 1882–89, vol. 4).

'8. Zazdrosna żona' [The envious wife], pp. 38–46 (Kolberg 1882–89, vol. 4).

'9. Wierna córka i żona' [The faithful daughter and wife], pp. 46–49 (Kolberg 1882–89, vol. 4).

'10. Brat i siostra' [The brother and the sister], pp. 49–53 (Kolberg 1882–89, vol. 4).

'11. Zamiana' [Substitution], pp. 53–58 (Kolberg 1882–89, vol. 4).

'12. Woda odmładniająca' [Youth-giving water], pp. 58–63 (Kolberg 1882–89, vol. 4), recorded near Horodenka town.

'13. Zdradliwa siostra' [The Insidious Sister], pp. 63–70 (Kolberg 1882–89, vol. 4), recorded in recorded in Spas and Myshyn villages.

'14. Zdradliwa siostra' [The Insidious Sister], pp. 70–73 (Kolberg 1882–89, vol. 4), recorded in Chortovets and Unizh villages.

'15. Zbójca i królewna' [The robber and the king's daughter], pp. 73–76 (Kolberg 1882–89, vol. 4), recorded near Obertyn village.

'16. Carówna wiarołomna' [The treacherous tsarivna], pp. 76–82 (Kolberg 1882–89, vol. 4), recorded near Horodenka town.

'17. Pogromca smoków' [The dragon slayer], pp. 82–92 (Kolberg 1882–89, vol. 4), recorded near Tlumach town.

'18. Królewna i pastuch' [The king's daughter and the shepherd], pp. 92–101 (Kolberg 1882–89, vol. 4), recorded in Hvizdets town and Soroky village [near Horodenka town?].

'19. Szewc i niedźwiedź' [The shoemaker and the bear], pp. 101–108 (Kolberg 1882–89, vol. 4), recorded in Spas and Myshyn villages.

'20. Szklanna góra' [The glass mountain], pp. 108–112 (Kolberg 1882–89, vol. 4), recorded in Horodnytsia village near Horodenka town.

'21. Złoty ptak i morska panna' [The golden bird and the sea maiden], pp. 112–108 (Kolberg 1882–89, vol. 4), recorded in Potochyshche village near Horodenka town.

'22. Szewczyk królem' [The son of shoemaker as the king], pp. 118–123 (Kolberg 1882–89, vol. 4), recorded in Horodnytsia village near Horodenka town.

'23. Kupiec i cesarzówna' [The merchant and the tsarivna], pp. 123–131 (Kolberg 1882–89, vol. 4), recorded in Spas and Myshyn villages.

'24. Cudowny koń' [The magic horse], pp. 131–140 (Kolberg 1882–89, vol. 4), recorded in Horodnytsia village near Horodenka town.

'25. Zamiana i jej skutki' [The substitution and its effects], pp. 141–144 (Kolberg 1882–89, vol. 4), recorded in Yaseniv-Pilnyi village near Horodenka town.

'26. Madejowe łoźe' [Madey's bed], pp. 145–149 (Kolberg 1882–89, vol. 4), recorded in Hvizdets town.

'27. Zboj Ywan' [Ivan the robber], pp. 149–154 (Kolberg 1882–89, vol. 4), recorded in Spas and Myshyn villages near Kolomyia town.

'28. Odbiór cyrografu' [Return of the promissory note], pp. 154–162 (Kolberg 1882–89, vol. 4), recorded in Horodnytsia village near Horodenka town.

'29. O chłopcu co spzedał czortowi swoja skórę' [About the young man who sold his skin to the *chort*], pp. 162–164 (Kolberg 1882–89, vol. 4), recorded in Horodnytsia village near Horodenka town.

'30. O chłopcu co się nikogo nie lekał' [About the young man who feared nothing], pp. 164–169 (Kolberg 1882–89, vol. 4), recorded near Horodenka town.

'31. Gazda' [The master], pp. 169–171 (Kolberg 1882–89, vol. 4), recorded in Hvizdets town.

'32. Czart i chléb' [The *chort* and the bread], pp. 171–173 (Kolberg 1882–89, vol. 4), near Hvizdets town.

'33. Poprawa skąpego księdza' [Improving a meagre priest], pp. 173–175 (Kolberg 1882–89, vol. 4), recorded in Strilche village near Horodenka town.

'34. Rozśmieszające przyrostki' [The amusing attachments], pp. 175–176 (Kolberg 1882–89, vol. 4), recorded in Spas and Kliuchiv [Velykyi Klyuchiv] villages.

'35. Syn niedźwiedzicy' [The bear's son], pp. 177–185 (Kolberg 1882–89, vol. 4), recorded in Pyadyky village, near Kolomyia town.

'36. Niewierna żona i wilkołak' [The unfaithful wife and the *vovkulaka*], pp. 185–190 (Kolberg 1882–89, vol. 4), recorded in Kolomyia town and Kliuchiv [Velykyi Klyuchiv] village.

'37. Tymko złodziej i diabli' [Tymko the thief and the *chorty*], pp. 190–194 (Kolberg 1882–89, vol. 4), recorded in Chortovets village.

'38. Cudowne byczki anielskie' [The angel's magic bulls], pp. 195–196 (Kolberg 1882–89, vol. 4), recorded in Horodnytsia village near Horodenka town.

'39. Sąd boży' [The judgment of God], pp. 197–198 (Kolberg 1882–89, vol. 4), recorded near Hvizdets town.

'40. Dwaj bracia' [Two brothers], pp. 198–200 (Kolberg 1882–89, vol. 4), recorded near Horodenka town.

'41. Anioł w służbie na ziemi' [The angel in service on earth], pp. 200–202 (Kolberg 1882–89, vol. 4), recorded in Kulachkivtsi village.

'42. Ksiądz co trzysta lat spał w niebie' [The priest slept in heaven for three hundred years], pp. 202–203 (Kolberg 1882–89, vol. 4), recorded in Horodenka town.

'43. Pasterstwo u św. Mikołaja' [Shepherding for Saint Nicholas], pp. 203–205 (Kolberg 1882–89, vol. 4), recorded in Kulachkivtsi village.

'44. Trzy przestrogi' [Three cautions], pp. 205–208 (Kolberg 1882–89, vol. 4), recorded near Horodenka town.

'45. Przygody znajdka' [Adventures of the foundling], pp. 208–210 (Kolberg 1882–89, vol. 4). (Kolberg omitted to indicate, where the folk tale was recorded.)

'46. Kara łakomstwa' [The punishment of gluttony], pp. 210–214 (Kolberg 1882–89, vol. 4), Yabluniv village, Kolomyia district.

'47. Bogacz i biedak' [The rich man and the poor man], pp. 214–216 (Kolberg 1882–89, vol. 4), recorded in Soroky village near Horodenka town.

'48. Mleko lekiem na oczy' [The milk as a cure for eye disease], pp. 216–219 (Kolberg 1882–89, vol. 4), recorded near Horodenka town.

'49. Trzy zagadki' [Three Riddles], pp. 220–224 (Kolberg 1882–89, vol. 4), recorded in Kulachkivtsi village.

'50. Mądra dziewka' [The wise maiden], pp. 224–226 (Kolberg 1882–89, vol. 4), recorded in Horodnytsia village near Horodenka town.

'51. Mądra dziewka: a variant' [The wise maiden: a variant], pp. 226–227 (Kolberg 1882–89, vol. 4), recorded in Hvizdets town.

'52. Łgarstwa' [Lies], pp. 112–108 (Kolberg 1882–89, vol. 4), recorded in Yaseniv-Pilnyi village near Horodenka town.

'53. O głuchej wsi: szereg nieporozumień' [About the deaf village: a series of misunderstandings], pp. 228–229 (Kolberg 1882–89, vol. 4), recorded in Verbyazh village, Kolomyia district.

'54. Durny syn' [The foolish son], pp. 229–230 (Kolberg 1882–89, vol. 4), recorded in Kolomyia town.

'55. Frant na franta' [The swindler against the swindler], pp. 230–232 (Kolberg 1882–89, vol. 4), recorded in Chortovets village.

'56. O durnym Hucule w wojsku' [About the foolish Hutsul soldier in the army], pp. 232–234 (Kolberg 1882–89, vol. 4), recorded in Kolomyia town.

'57. Trzej bracia' [Three brotehrs], pp. 235–237 (Kolberg 1882–89, vol. 4), recorded in Kulachkivtsi village.

'58. Trzej synowie' [Three sons], pp. 237–238 (Kolberg 1882–89, vol. 4), recorded in Kulachkivtsi village.

'59. Dobry nabytek' [The good purchase], pp. 238–241 (Kolberg 1882–89, vol. 4), recorded nea9 Horodenka town.

'60. Dobra sprzedaź' [The good sale], pp. 241–243 (Kolberg 1882–89, vol. 4), recorded in Pyadyky village.

'61. Przebiegły szewc' [The Shoemaker and the Bear], pp. 243–246 (Kolberg 1882–89, vol. 4), recorded in Hvizdets town.

'62. Złodziej u spowiedzi' [The thief in confession], pp. 246–247 (Kolberg 1882–89, vol. 4), recorded near Horodenka town.

'63. Skradziona rewerenda' [The stolen priest's cloak], pp. 247–248 (Kolberg 1882–89, vol. 4), recorded in Horodenka town.

'64. Skradziony kożuch' [The stolen kozhukh], p. 248 (Kolberg 1882–89, vol. 4), recorded in Horodenka town.

'65. Gazda i trzej zalotnicy' [The Shoemaker and the Bear], pp. 248–250

(Kolberg 1882–89, vol. 4), recorded in Sniatyn town.

'66. Gazdyni i dijak' [The mistress and the deacon], pp. 250–252 (Kolberg 1882–89, vol. 4), recorded in Horodenka town.

'67. Dijak przez męźa zduszony' [The deacon strangled by the husband], pp. 252–253 (Kolberg 1882–89, vol. 4), Turka village, near Kolomyia town.

'68. Przygody chłopca' [Adventures of the boy], pp. 253–258 (Kolberg 1882–89, vol. 4), recorded in Obertyn and Chortovets villages.

'69. Baba czterykroć grzebiona' [The old woman, who was buried four times], pp. 258–261 (Kolberg 1882–89, vol. 4), recorded in Horodenka town.

'70. Koza' [The goat], pp. 262–266 (Kolberg 1882–89, vol. 4), recorded in Spas and Myshyn villages.

'71. Pies i Wilk' [The dog and the wolf], pp. 266–268 (Kolberg 1882–89, vol. 4), recorded near Horodenka town.

'72. Osiol, niedzwiedz i wilk' [The donkey, the bear and the wolf], pp. 268–270 (Kolberg 1882–89, vol. 4), recorded in Horodenka town.

'73. Koszałki-opałki: kazka-prykazka i durna nebylycia' [Koshalky–Opalky: nonsense verse and tall tale], pp. 271–280 (Kolberg 1882–89, vol. 4), recorded in Zhabye and Iltsi villages.

'74. Kazka zá dyjamentowu dorohu' [The fairy tale about the diamond road], pp. 280–286 (Kolberg 1882–89, vol. 4), recorded in Zhabye and Iltsi villages.

'75. Łegin co piecem za wodą chodził' [The young man with pich went for water], pp. 286–290 (Kolberg 1882–89, vol. 4), recorded in Zhabye and Iltsi villages.

'76. Kazka za czemnoho kusznieria' [A fairy tale about a polite furrier], pp. 290–292 (Kolberg 1882–89, vol. 4), recorded in Zhabye and Iltsi villages.

'77. Za cikawoho pesyka: co rozsmiesza smutna cesarzownę' [About the amusing dog, which made a sad tsarivna laugh], pp. 292–294 (Kolberg 1882–89, vol. 4), recorded in Zhabye and Iltsi villages.

PART 2

MOSZYNSKA's Collection

About Moszynska's Collection

In volume 9 of *Zbior Wiadomosci*, Josefa Moszynska published her collection of Ukrainian folk tales and riddles (Moszynska 1885). The collection includes a total of 37 folk tales and 156 riddles.

At the end of the volume, a brief note states that, with one exception, all the folk tales were recorded by Josefa Moszynska from women in Tarashcha county and Vasylkiv county [in the Kyiv province].

The riddles and especially the folk tales represent a valuable contribution to the current literature on the subject. Due to the limited awareness of Josefa Moszynska's collection, I have provided brief summaries of all the folk tales included and added bibliographic notes, particularly as none were included in her original collection.

Josefa Moszynska's folk tales are compelling from both historical and literary perspectives. Overall, the collection is remarkable for its content, completeness, and the significance of its versions of the folk tales.

2.1. About Marko the Rich

_⌃_

Comments: This is an expanded version of the folk tales found in Pavlo Chubynsky's collection (Chubynsky 1872–78, vol. 2, pp. 341–344) and in Petro Ivanov's article on Ukrainian legends (Ivanov 1890–93).

Moszynska's version introduces the following motif: Marko sends his son-in-law to the Hellish *Had* [Engl., 'Serpent'] to determine when it is more profitable to trade – early or late in the day.

I published a detailed article about Marko the Rich in vol. 20 of *The Ethnographic Review* (Sumtsov 1894a) , with a supplement in vol. 21 (Sumtsov 1894b).

Book cover of Marko the Rich, *published in Uzhhorod in 1922 by Prosvita Society as part of 'Tales for Young Children' series, no. 3.*

2.2. About the Fortunate Fool

This tale is about three brothers, with the youngest being the simpleton. All three brothers propose marriage to the Tsar's daughter, and it is the youngest who succeeds, aided by *Skorokhid* (Swiftwalker), *Obyidalo* (Devour-it-all) and *Obpyvailo* (Drink-it-all), who fulfil the Tsar's tasks.

_⌃_

Comments: Folk tales with this motif appear in the folklore of various cultures. I have listed relevant bibliography on this topic in my review of Romanov's *Belarusian Collection* (Sumtsov 1894e).

Additionally, see my comments on '1.18. The King's Daughter and the Shepherd' on page 41.

Illustration by E. W. Mitchell for the Ukrainian fairy tale 'The Tsar and the Angel', a version of '2.14. About Iohan the Tsar' (Bain 1894, p. 169).

2.3. About Three Brothers

A poor man had three sons; the youngest was a simpleton. They went off to work. After serving an old man for a year, the eldest son earned a table that could provide all kinds of food.

However, on his way back home, a stranger replaced it with an ordinary table and kept the magic one for himself. The second son earned a gold-horned ram that produced money, but the same stranger stole that ram too. The youngest son, the simpleton, earned a self-beating stick. When the stranger tried to take the stick, it sprang to life and began to beat him, forcing him to return all three stolen items to the brothers.

_–^–_

Comments: The French and other Western [European] versions of the tale are presented in Cosquin's *Collection* (1886, vol. 1, pp. 51–59, no. 4 and pp. 237–246, no. 22; & vol. 2, pp. 51–59, no. 39, pp. 79–88, no. 42, pp. 107–114, no. 56, & pp. 124–127, no. 59).

See other Ukrainian folk tales with this motif in:

Manzhura (1890, pp. 70–71 & 74–76); and Rudchenko (1869–70, vol. 2, pp. 125–136, no. 31);

Polish:

Chelchowski (1890–91, vol. 1, pp. 166–171 & 238–246);
Zawilinski (1889, pp. 53, 54 & 67–74); and Ciszewski (1894, pp. 168–170, no. 122);

Russian:

Sadovnikov (1884, pp. 73–77, no. 12);

Belarusian:

Dobrovolskiy (1891, pp. 693–696, no. 12 (cf. my comments on '1.4. The Magic Stone' on page 29 and '1.22. The Son of Shoemaker as the King' on page 47).

Ivan Bilyk (Ivan Rudchenko; 1845–1905) (left) a Ukrainian folklorist, ethnographer, writer, translator, and literary critic, with his younger brother and co-author, Panas Myrnyi (right).

2.4. About the Abducted Boy

_^_

Comments: The tale consists of three intertwined motifs:

(1) Kidnapping – The Tatars abducted a boy with the intent to eat him but spared him due to his strikingly handsome appearance. The boy was tasked with cooking all kinds of herbs for them, and one day, after tasting the herbs, he began to understand the language of animals and plants.

(2) *Pesyholovtsi* [Dog-headed] – The young man escaped from the Tatars but was soon captured by the *Pesyholovtsi*, a group of cannibalistic creatures. Through cunning, he burned their cook – who had been roasting people in the oven – and managed to flee.

(3) Tsardom of the Underworld – The young man eventually found himself in the Tsardom of the Underworld,[26] where he lived with a wealthy Moorish woman. However, he soon missed his homeland and escaped.

Each of these motifs is explored in greater detail in other tales, such as:

(1) Kidnapping – Yastrebov 1894, pp. 134–135, no. 8;

(2) *Pesyholovtsi* – Literature on the *Pesyholovtsi* is extensive and will not be discussed here, see: Buslaev (1861), Veselovskiy's works, Kolberg, (1882–89, vol. 3), Chubynsky (1872–78), Yastrebov (1894, pp. 80–83), and others.

26. Tsardom of the Underworld – 'підземне царство', sometimes referred to simply as 'underworld' in the texts.

(3) Tsardom of the Underworld – For more on this motif, see my article 'Sketches on A. Pushkin' (Sumtsov 1893c).

2.5. Hen the Riaba

The poor man found his lazy *Dolia* [Fate] in the forest and, after giving her a good beating, took from her a speckled hen [hence the title 'Hen the Riaba'] that laid precious stones for him. When a villain discovered this, he deceived the hen's owner's wife, convincing her to slaughter the hen. She killed and cooked it; her eldest son ate the head and became a wise, all-knowing man, while the younger son ate the liver and giblets and became extremely rich. On the villain's advice, their mother prepared poison for both sons, but they managed to escape.

The elder brother later attended the election of the Tsar; a dove landed on his head [three] times, and he was chosen as Tsar. The younger brother married the daughter of another Tsar, but she soon killed him. The elder brother revived him with life-giving water and, as punishment, turned his murderous wife into a donkey and had her dismembered by horses in the field.

_^_

Comments: The main motifs of this folk tale, often found separately, are: (1) catching one's *Dolia* [Fate], (2) the insidious wife, and (3) the miraculous election of the Tsar. Each of these motifs appears in numerous historical legends and folk tales. Here are a few examples:

(1) Catching one's *Dolia* [Fate]:

Manzhura (1890, pp. 49, 52–54 [about *Dolia*] & 60 [about *Bida*]);

Chubynsky (1872–78, vol. 5, p. 10–16);

Carnoy & Nicolaides (1889, pp. 43–57, no. 2); and

Hahn (1864, vol. 1, no. 36 (here, Fate was caught by its hair).

Ancient Egyptians held similar beliefs, as noted by Maspero (1889, p. lxv).

(2) The insidious wife: see my comments on '1.16. The Treacherous Tsarivna' on page 39.

(3) The miraculous election of the Tsar: I briefly discussed this motif in my article on the 'mouse' character in folklore (Sumtsov 1891), and will examine it in more detail in a forthcoming monograph. Among Russian scholars, academic A. Veselovskiy, who touched upon the motif in his review of Scheflfer's works (Veselovskiy 1868) and in his research on South–Russian [Ukrainian] epics (Veselovskiy 1881).

This motif is particularly fascinating as it appears in relation to various historical and semi-historical figures, such as Peter the Great (in a Georgian folk tale), Przemysl, etc.

2.6. About the Merciful Lad

The son of a poor widow bought a kitten, a puppy, and a snakelet, rescuing them from people who were beating them. The animals later performed great services for him. In gratitude for rescuing her snakelet, the mother snake gave the young man a magic ring that fulfilled its owner's every wish.

The young man had a palace built for himself and married the Tsarivna. However, the Tsarivna soon fell out of love with him, stole his ring, and turned him into a pillar. The kitten and puppy managed to steal the ring back from the Tsarivna, but on their way to their master, they dropped it into the sea. The kitten then began to torment tadpoles, prompting their mother to command the frogs to retrieve the ring. The ring was recovered, and its owner turned his wife into a pillar as punishment, then restored her to human form. Afterwards, they lived together in love and harmony.

_-^-_

Comments:

(1) Grateful animals – This motif is widespread across various cultures and belongs to an extensive group of folk tales about grateful animals, often mentioned in groups of three. An analogous Halychyna-Rus (Hutsul) version appears in Kolberg's collection (1882–89, vol. 3,

Illustration for 'The Brother and Sister in the Forest,' featuring 'grateful animals' (Rudchenko, 1920c, p. 11).

no. 74, while a Polish version is found in *Lud*, (Kolberg 1857–90, vol. 3, pp. 139–142, no. 12). I also list several references to the motif of grateful animals in my comments on '1.11. The Substitution [1]' on page 34; '1.12. The Youth-Giving Water' on page 34 & '1.13 & 1.14. The Insidious Sister' on page 36.

(2) The lost ring – This second motif is also common in many Eastern and Western folk tales. A modern Greek tale in Carnoy & Nicolaides (1889, p. 70, no. 3 & p. 203, no. 6) is especially similar to this Ukrainian folk tale.

2.7. Pokotyhoroshko

A woman ate a pea and gave birth to a son, *Pokotyhoroshko*[27]. He quickly grew up, became strong, and set out into the world. Along the way, he met *Vernydub* (Pull-up-the-Oak) and *Vernyhora* (Turn-the-Mountain) who became

27. Pokotyhoroshko = Kotyhoroshko = 'Roll-a-Pea'

his companions. *Pokotyhoroshko* rescued the *Tsarivna* from the *Zmiy* [Serpent], but *Vernydub* and *Vernyhora* abducted her from him.

During the rainstorm, *Pokotyhoroshko* sheltered the nestlings of the *Zhar-Ptytsia* [Firebird] with his clothes. In gratitude, the *Zhar-Ptytsia* carried him back to his homeland. Once there, he killed *Vernydub*, and took his *Tsarivna* away from *Vernyhora* and married her.

_^_

Comments: Similar versions can be found in the collections of Chubynsky (1872–78, vol. 2, pp. 229–239) and Kolberg (1882–89, vol. 4, pp. 280–286). For additional references, see my comments on the folk tales: '1.18. The King's Daughter and the Shepherd' on page 41, '1.74. The Fairy Tale about the Diamond Road' on page 88, and '1.75. About the Lazy Son' on page 88.

The title of the folk tale, 'Pokotyhoroshko', became quite popular in Ukraine, and most of the Ukrainian tales on the theme of the miraculous conception in various collections are recorded under this title.

2.8. Brother the Little Ram

A brother and sister set out into the world. The sister warned her brother not to drink from wells where oxen, horses, and sheep had drunk. Twice he obeyed, but on the third occasion, he drank from such a well and was transformed into a little ram.

The sister married a *Pan* and gave birth to a son. Her brother, the little ram, took care of the child. While bathing in a river with her mistress, the maid drowned the sister, stole her dress, and pretended to be her mistress. The drowned woman transformed into a duck and continued to visit the riverbank to feed her child, with the little ram bringing him there. Eventually, the impostor ordered the duck to be slaughtered. From the duck's blood, two golden trees grew, but on the impostor's orders, they were cut down.

A splinter from the trees fell into an old woman's chest and transformed back into the ram's sister. She secretly cleaned the rooms at night until the old woman noticed and informed the *Pan*. Upon learning the truth, the *Pan* ordered the impostor to be dismembered by horses in the field – a common conclusion in many versions of this folk tale.

This version, however, includes a unique addition:

'Where her [the impostor's] head fell,
A grave mound appeared;
Where her shoulders touched,
A valley was formed.'

This type of ending is also found in folk songs and legends, including the 'Kalevala'.

_^_

Comments: The tales about Brother the Little Ram have various titles across collections; for example, 'The Three-Year Old Calf' in Chubynsky's collection (1872–78, vol. 2).[28]

Versions of this folk tale appear in the collections of:
Manzhura (1890, p. 15);
Sadovnikov (1884, pp. 218–222, no. 65);
Khudiakov (1860–62, vol. 2, pp. 85–87, no. 61);
Lominadze (1894, pp. 40 & 43);

Miller (his reviews of the Caucasian collections);[29] Ciszewski (1894, pp. 89–97, no. 75); and Cosquin (1886, vol. 1, pp. 60–81, no. 5 & pp. 246–254, no. 23; includes French and other Western [European] folk tales).

28. Incomplete or incorrect citation in the original.

29. Incomplete or incorrect citation in the original.

Notably, similar tales existed among the ancient Egyptians as recorded by Maspero (1889, no. 1). Such tales remain popular among various distant peoples, for instance, the Zulu (Koropchevskiy 1874, p. 60).

'Kullervo's Curse' by Akseli Gallen-Kallela (1899).

'Rus peasants from Hermakivka village, Chortkiv county, eastern Halychyna',
(Holovatsky 1878, vol. 3, p. 1).

2.9. The Wicked Stepmother and Her Daughter

A weak-willed father, under pressure from his second wife (the stepmother of his daughter), took his daughter to the *Zmiy's* house in the forest. Along the way, the daughter performed acts of kindness for a mouse, a tree, a *pich*, and a water well.

At the *Zmiy's* request, she carried him over the threshold, prepared his supper, washed his head, made his bed, and rang the bell over his head [throughout the night to help him sleep]. When she grew tired, the mouse came to her aid. In gratitude, the *Zmiy* gave her valuable gifts, and she returned home wealthy.

The stepmother, hoping for similar riches, sent her own daughter to the *Zmiy*. However, the latter refused to help the mouse, the tree, and the other entities. She failed to complete the *Zmiy's* challenges. Although she attempted to take horses with golden bridles when leaving, they vanished upon her arrival home, and she fell gravely ill.

_^_

Comments: This folk tale is well documented in the collections of:

Afanasiev (1873 [?]); and

Carnoy & Nicolaides (1889, pp. 127–144, no. 7).

[Ukrainian versions of this tale] often feature the Mare's Head instead of *Zmiy*: see 'Comments' to '1.3 The Daughter and the Stepdaughter (2)' on page 28.

Illustration by E. W. Mitchell, for the Ukrainian fairy tale 'Ivan Golik [Holyk] and the Serpents' (Bain 1894, p. 281).

2.10. About Suchych

The *Tsarytsia* had no children. Following an old man's advice, she ate a fish to conceive a child. Her cook tasted some of the fish, and her dog ate the discarded bones. As a result, the *Tsarytsia*, the cook, and the dog each gave birth to a boy: *Tsarevych* [the Tsar's son], *Kuharevych* [the cook's son], and *Suchych* [the dog's son]. Together, the three boys performed various feats.

They shot arrows to determine their paths and travelled in those directions. *Suchych* went to rescue three sisters, *Tsarivny*, who had been taken captive by the *Zmiyi*. He successfully defeated their captors.

_–^–_

Comments: This folk tale contains several intriguing motifs:

(1) The motif of the whip and mittens as token of distress – *Suchych* left his whip and mittens at home, instructing *Kuharevych* and *Tsarevych* to come to his aid if blood dripped from the whip or foam appeared on the mittens.

(2) The motif of throwing the boot – During his battle with the

'Volynian women' by Leon Zienkowicz (1841).

nine-headed *Zmiy*, *Suchych* threw his boot into the stable, breaking nine metal doors to free his horse, which ultimately helped him defeat the *Zmiy*.

The middle part of this folk tale often appears as a separate tale, where the *Zmiy* pursues *Suchych*. He seeks refuge at *Kuzma-Demyan's* forge. *Kuzma-Demyan* grabs the *Zmiy's* tongue with tongs, harnesses him to a plough, and ploughs the field to the sea.[30]

The ending is also commonly retold independently. In this version, *Suchych* asks for the *Tsarivna's* hand in marriage. The Tsar sets an enormous feast, which *Suchych* manages with the help of *Obyidalo* (Devour-it-All), *Obpyvalo* (Drink-it-All),. Occasionally, two other helpers appear: *The One Who Coils Water onto the Swift* (retrieves the ring from the sea) and *The One Who Sets His Eyes onto the Pitchfork and Sees Everything in the Sky* (brings the *Tsarivna* down from the heavens, where she is hiding).

30. This legend and its variations are believed to explain the origins of *Zmiyevi Valy* (English: the Serpent's Wall), an ancient system of earthwork fortifications.

Similar folk tales are discussed in my comments on '1.18. The King's Daughter and the Shepherd' on page 41.

Suchych, as a folk tale hero, has drawn scholarly attention. Potebnia provided valuable insights in his review of Chubynsky's *Collection* (1872–78, vol. 2, pp. 40–45 & pp. 252–269) and in his work *On the History of the Sounds* (Potebnia 1881).

The motif of throwing the boot in 'About Suchych' is reminiscent of the 'Chobotok' tale in Kallash (1890, p. 256).

The tragic sign of blood dripping from a whip recurs in many other folk tales, such as Hahn (1864, vol. 1, no. 18) and Cosquin (1886, vol. 1, pp. 60–81, no. 5).

The archaic practice of determining one's path by the flight of an arrow is also found in:

Manzhura (1890, pp. 11–14, 21–22 & 24–27);

Karadžić (1870, pp. 208–212, no. 3); and

Cosquin (1886, vol. 1, pp. 133–154, no. 12).

2.11. The Old Man's Goats

Comments: This folk tale is a variation of '1.70. About the Old Man's Goats' on page 82 (Kolberg 1882–89, vol. 4, pp. 262–266). References to similar folk tales are also provided there.

Illustration for the Ukrainian fairy tale 'Koza-Dereza' (Vovk, 1921, p. 4).

Illustration for the Ukrainian fairy tale 'Koza-Dereza' (Pavlovych, 1921, p. 6).

Illustration for the Ukrainian fairy tale 'Koza-Dereza'(Lukashevych, 1909, pp. 80, 82 & 84)

2.12. About the Murdered Sister

Three sisters lived together: one was beautiful, and the other two were not. Driven by envy, the two ugly sisters murdered the beautiful one in the forest. A lira-player, mistaking her remains for those of a slain lamb (sic), used her intestines to craft strings for his lira.

When played, the lira's strings sang: 'Unhurriedly, old man, play…' and revealed the truth about the murdered maiden and her sisters, the murderers. The lira sang the same tale to the maiden's father: 'Unhurriedly, father, play…' and finally to her brother. Terrified by the song, the brother dropped the lira, and its strings transformed back into the maiden. The treacherous sisters were then imprisoned.

_⌃_

Comments: This folk tale is widely known, with similar versions appearing as songs. It is likely that these folk tales originated from such songs, as most versions retain song-like elements. Comprehensive

'A lira-player', Zhivopisnaya Rossiya, *1897, vol. 5, p. 42.*

references on folk tales and songs about the prophetic flute can be found in: Child, (1882–98, vol. 1 no. 10; and supplements to vol. 2, p. 495, vol. 4, p. 498, vol. 6, p. 499 & vol. 8, p. 447) and in a special study by Biegeleisen (*Wisla*, 1893, vol. 7, nos. 2 & 3) [31].

31. Incomplete or incorrect citation in the original.

Similar Ukrainian folk tales:

> Kulish (1856–57, vol. 2, p. 20);
> Manzhura (1890, p. 58); and
> Rudchenko (1869 –70, vol. 1, pp. 156–158, no. 55).

Russian and Belarusian versions of the folk tale are in:

> Khudiakov (1860–62, vol. 2, pp. 75–78, no. 57);
> Sadovnikov (1884, pp. 105–108, no. 21);
> Afanasiev (1873 [?]); and
> Dobrovolskiy (1891, p. 560–561, no. 26).

Sheet music for a song akin to this folk tale, titled Folk Tale About a Magic Sopilka *(pp. 34–37), in which an envious brother kills his younger sibling. The lyrics include: 'Unhurriedly, unhurriedly, chumak, play. Don't let my heart fade away. My brother killed me. He buried me in the orchard – and all because of that boar.' (p. 35).*

2.13. The Pipe of Endless Tobacco, the Gold–Giving Purse, and the Self–Grabbing Sack

A discharged soldier offered food to an old man traveling along the road, who turned out to be God in disguise. In gratitude, God gave the soldier three magic objects: the pipe with endless tobacco (*pipe-nevykurka*), the gold-giving purse (*purse-zolotodayka*), and the self-grabbing sack (*sack-samokhvat*).

'Soldier and Death' by Taras Shevchenko (1844).

Later, the soldier employed the sack to trap the *chorty* that had made his home uninhabitable. Finally, he used the sack to imprison Smert [Death]. When he eventually released Smert, she was so terrified of him that she refused to take him, thus making him immortal.

Weary of eternal life, the soldier went to hell, but the *chorty* rejected him. He then sought refuge in heaven, where he quarrelled with the Apostle Peter and trapped him in the self-grabbing sack. God later freed Peter and, as punishment, confined the soldier in the self-grabbing sack until the Last Judgment.

_^_

Comments: This folk tale blends two prominent legendary motifs:

(1) Man's temporary domination over death – This motif appears in:

Shapkarev (1892–94, vol. 8, pp. 392–396, no. 241);

Carnoy & Nicolaides (1889, p. 172, no. 8 & p. 144, no. 11);

Karadžić (1870, pp. 144–147, no. 37);

Sadovnikov (1884, pp. 266–268, no. 88, pp. 272–282, no. 92 & pp. 309–312, no. 104);

Ivanov (1890–93, book 7, p. 84); and

Potanin (1881–83, issue 4, p. 498–499, no. 142).

(2) The soldier's visits to hell and heaven – Variations of this motif are found in:

Dobrovolskiy (1891, p. 285–286, no. 51);

Ulanowska (1884, p. 301);

Zhytetskyi (1893, p. 98);

Afanasiev (1793);

Ciszewski (1894, pp. 168–170, no. 122); and

Kryptadia, vol. 2, p. 77, etc.[32]

32. Sumtsov's comments include two incomplete or incorrect references: Geyer's article in *The Collection of Statistical Materials of the Syr-Darya Region* and *Kyivan Antiquity*.

2.14. About Iohan the Tsar

This is an extraordinary legend.

Iohan the Tsar was healthy, rich, and happy. However, in a moment of arrogance, he declared, 'God and I are the same. God matters no more than I do.'

Three months later, while hunting, he spotted a golden-horned

deer and chased it relentlessly. The deer ran into a lake, and Iohan the Tsar, removing his clothes, followed it into the water. Suddenly, the deer and his clothes vanished. The deer was, in fact, an Angel in disguise. The Angel then donned the Tsar's robes and took his place, ruling in his stead.

No one recognised the true Tsar – not his loyal dogs, nor his horse, nor his courtiers; even the Tsarytsia failed to recognise him. Beaten and driven away from the palace, Iohan found refuge in a monk's cell, where he repented for his arrogance. Once he had truly atoned, the Angel returned his clothes, and everyone immediately recognised and welcomed him back.

_^_

Comments: This tale includes two captivating motifs:

(1) The shape-shifting Deer-Angel.

I briefly touched upon this motif in 'Cultural Experiences' (Sumtsov 1889). The motif of the deer is deeply embedded in legends, folk tales, and songs. This Ukrainian tale resembles the Georgian folk tales recorded in Teptsov (1894, p. 15) and Mashurko (1894, p. 250).

(2) The hubristic Tsar.

This motif originates in Eastern traditions and is found in tales about Solomon (Margolin 1880, p. 9) and other heroes. Similar versions appear in:

Cosquin (1886, vol. 1, pp. 133–152, no. 12, pp. 186–200, no. 17 & pp. 208–221, no. 19);
Veselovskiy (1886, p. 298);
Manzhura (1890, pp. 40–43);
Ciszewski (1894, pp. 35–37, no. 48);
Shapkarev (1892–94, vol. 8, p. 146–149, no. 97);
Eivazov (1894, p. 99);
Bezhanov (1894, pp. 148 & 194); etc.

A version of '2.14. About Iohan the Tsar', titled 'The Arrogant Tsar' appears in Ivan Rudchenko's collection (1920b), accompanied by Yuriy Mahalevsky illustration, depicting the Tsar being visited by an Angel.

2.15. About the Chumak's Daughter

Three young men sought the hand of the same maiden [the *Chumak's* daughter]. She promised to marry all three but then hid from them in a pit. A pig and a dog later fell into the pit and transformed into maidens. The young men, unaware of this, ended up marrying these three women.

Rude and unkempt people were said to have originated from the Woman the Pig, evil people from the Woman the Dog, and good people from the *Chumak's* daughter.

_^_

Comments: This folk tale appears to be original. Somewhat similar tales are found in Manzhura (1890) [...].

'Chumak' by Kostiantyn Trutovskyi (circa 1850-s)

2.16. About the Rich Man in a Village

A rich man went into the forest to hide his money, while a poor man went there to cut twigs for a new broom. A *chort*, disguised as a *Panych*, helped the poor man gather the twigs and then brought him the money from the rich man's hidden cauldron.

When the rich man discovered his treasure was gone, he was devastated. The *chort* handed him a rope, which the rich man used to hang himself.

_^_

Comments: This folk tale is unique, with only slight similarities to tales about two brothers and *Zlydni*.

'Vakula Flying on a Chort' by M. Tkachenko (1911), illustration for M. Hohol's novel 'The Night Before Christmas'.

2.17. About the Robbers

A group of robbers wooed a rich peasant's daughter and took her into the forest. The robbers' maid warned her that they killed their wives and showed her the bodies of their victims. Terrified, the young woman fled. Along the way, she first hid in a tree and later concealed herself in hay on a cart.

The three pursuing robbers wounded her twice in the leg with a spear during their search but ultimately failed to find her. Upon reaching her father's house, they were captured.

_^_

Comments: I will publish a separate study on folk tales featuring this motif in my upcoming article, 'Sketches on A. Pushkin' [cf. Sumtsov 1893c & 1894c]. This study will also include an analysis of Pushkin's poem 'Zhenikh' (The Bridegroom), so I will not elaborate further here to avoid repetition.

'Ukrainian woman-reaper' by Shubeler, published in Niva, *no. 48, p. 761.*

'The second battle of Dobrynia and Zmiy' (Avenarius, 1876, p. 59). More on Dobrynia see '1.21. The Golden Bird and the Sea Tsarivna' on page 44.

2.18. What Is Destined Will Come to Pass

A beggar foretold to a peasant that he would receive fifty lashes. [In an attempt to escape his destiny,] the peasant immured himself in a *pich*, leaving only a small hole for breathing. However, the *Pan's* bird flew in through the hole, and the peasant accidently crushed it. The *Pan's* servants discovered him, dragged him out, and gave him the fifty lashes as foretold.

—∧—

33. Incomplete or incorrect citation in the original.

34. Incomplete or incorrect citation in the original.

Comments: The motif [of foretelling one's fortune] is common in many legends and folk tales. Examples include:

Bulgarian tales in: *The Collection of Folk Tales* (Sapundzhiev 1891);

An ancient [Kyivan] Rus legend about Oleh the Prophet and similar legends in Sukhomlynov's article in *Osnova* (1862);

Polish tales in: *Wisla* 1890[33]; and

Serbian tales in: *Znanie* 1877, no. 59[34].

ΙΙΜΑΚΑΙΙΙΑΙΦ ἐΒCΗΠΛΑΤΕΒΕΝΙCΑ . ΗΜΕCΩΑΗΓΓΟΤΡΙΒ ΟΙΙΑΡΙΙ
Ηгорь . ἐЖΕΓΛΠΤb ΓΑΨΕCΟΒΗЦΑ. ἐ ΗΚΙΜΟΓΗΛΑ Ἐ ΗΔ ο ῖΕΔ ΛΗ · Ϫο

The year 912: At the remains of his beloved horse where Kniaz Oleh or Oleh the Prophet was fatally bitten by a snake. (The Radziwill Chronicle).

2.19. About the Foolish and Lazy Wife

There was a woman who refused to clean the barrels, reap the crops, or fetch firewood from the forest. She spent all her time idling. One night, while she was sleeping, her husband took her *sorochka* and left with it.

When she awoke and went outside, she noticed thieves in the barn. To avoid being seen, she hid in a barrel filled with feathers. Later, as she wandered into the garden, her appearance caused people to mistake her for a *chort*. They sent for the priest, but he fell off a bridge into the river. In the end, the husband took his foolish wife back.

'After Bathing' by K. Trutovskyi (1890); featuring a girl in a sorochka.

_^_

Comments: A similar Ukrainian folk tale is included in the collection of Manzhura (1890).

2.20. About Two Comrades and the Wicked Wife

Two comrades married their betrothed: one had a kind and good-natured wife, while the other had a wicked wife who constantly scolded and beat him. When his comrade came to visit, he witnessed how, despite his friend performing all the household duties – even cooking *borshch* – his wife still beat him.

To deceive her, the visiting comrade falsely claimed that his own wife forced him to carry her in a sack until she fell asleep. Inspired by this tale, the wicked wife ordered her husband to sew a sack and carry her in it. However, her husband acted shrewdly: while she was in the sack, he gave her a sound thrashing. After this, the couple began to live amicably.

_^_

Comments: A similar Bulgarian folk tale is included in *The Collection of Folk Tales* (Pamukchiev 1891). A Ukrainian version of the tale can be found in Yastrebov's collection (1894, pp. 170–171, no. 31).

2.21. About the Woman Who Outsmarted the Chort and Beat Him

[The woman and the *chort* entered into a deal to grow crops together and share the harvest.] The first time, they grew turnips, and the woman claimed the roots for herself, leaving the foliage for the *chort*. The next time, they grew millet, and she took the foliage, leaving the roots for the *chort*.

[Angered by her trickery,] the *chort* began to fight with her across the fence, using a pitchfork while the woman wielded a stake. The pitchfork became stuck in the fence, and the woman struck the *chort* with the stake, forcing him to flee.

_^_

Comments: This folk tale is widely known and popular among various cultures:

Ukrainian: Rudchenko (1869–70, vol. 1, pp. 52–54, no. 29);

The Caucasus people: *Collection of Materials for Describing the Caucasus*[35];

Serbs: Karadžić (1870, pp. 274–277, no. 20);

35. Incomplete or incorrect citation in the original.

Detail of I. Prianishnikov's illustration (1874-76) from M. Hohol's novel 'The Lost Letter'; featuring chorty.

Bulgarians: Shapkarev (1892–94, vol. 8, p. 93–94, no. 74);

36. Incomplete citation in the original.

French: *Revue des Traditions Populaires* (1889, no. 9)[36], and among isolated coastal communities (Basset, Rene, p. 137)[37].

37. Incorrect citation in the original.

2.22. About the Woman who Shaved the Chort

An old peasant struck a deal to hand over his wife to the *chort*. The woman, displeased with the shaggy and long-haired creature, decided to groom him: she poured boiling water over his head and attempted to shave him with a plough's coulter. Terrified, the *chort* fled, and the peasant offered him shelter from his wife.

The *chort* then began tormenting the priest, the *Pan's* housekeeper, and the estate manager. Pretending to cure them, the peasant visited each one, and the *chort* left them in peace. The peasant received payment for his supposed healing services.

Later, the *Pan* fell ill and demanded the peasant's help, but the peasant refused, remembering the deal he had made with the *chort* – that the *chort* would leave only three patients unharmed. The peasant was brought by force, but just as the *chort* was about to attack him, the peasant summoned his wife. Terrified, the *chort* fled without looking back.

_^_

Comments: Many versions of this folk tale have the *chort* [devil] replaced with Smert [Death]. Professor A. Veselovskiy referenced this motif extensively in his article on the 'Indifferent Ones' in the afterlife, as seen in Dante's Inferno (Veselovskiy 1888). Additionally, motifs involving Smert [Death] as a *kuma* and the peasant-doctor appear in:

Shapkarev (1892–94, pp. 392–396, no. 241);
Carnoy & Nicolaides (1889, p. 144, no. 8 & p. 171 no. 11);
Ivanov (1890–93, book 5, pp. 142–154);
Stoikov (1891, p. 162);
Singer (1892, p. 299; (contains a valuable reference to a similar Talmudic legend);
Dobrovolskiy (1891, pp. 311–316, no. 10); and
Potanin (1881–83, issue 4, p. 498–499, no. 142).

2.23. About the Propasnytsia and the Peasant

38. Petro Yefymenko, in his collection of Ukrainian spells mentions a spell to cure jaundice; and there chimney is also used in the treatment ceremony. The collection also includes spells to treat *Propasnytsia*. (see Yefymenko 2020).

A peasant overheard three *Propasnytsi* [Fevers] talking. One said she tormented a priest, another tormented a Jew, and the third tormented a Gypsy. One of them revealed that she planned to torment the peasant by entering his body with the first spoonful of peas he ate.

The peasant hurried home, tied up the first spoonful of peas in a pouch, and hung it in the chimney. For an entire year, the *Propasnytsia* shook and suffered in the smoke.[38]

_^_

Comments: This tale is unique but bears some resemblance to the folk tale about *Zlydni*. Interestingly, records from the 17th–18th centuries on witchcraft, published by Volodymyr Antonovych (1877) as the appendix to Pavlo Chubynsky's *Works* (Chubynsky 1872–78), include a similar story documented in a judicial register on witchcraft.

2.24. About Baba the Whisperer

A woman's husband died, leaving her in dire poverty with twelve children. A priest taught her to 'whisper' [recite incantations] and instructed her to say:

> 'After a prayer, say this:
> If you provide money – it will help;
> If you provide bread – it will help;
> If you provide *salo* – it will help;
> If it helps – glory to God,
> But if it doesn't help, damn you.'

The woman began performing this whisper for people, and her fame grew. Over time, she became wealthy.

One day, the priest developed an abscess on his throat and called the *baba-whisperer* for help. When he heard her incantation and recognised her, he laughed so loudly that the abscess burst, and he recovered.

_∧_

Comments: I heard two versions of this tale in the Kharkiv province. One is nearly identical to this version. In the other version, a monkey replaced the *baba-whisperer*, and a clerk, the monkey's owner, replaced the priest.[39]

39. The use of laughter as a treatment for an abscess is also referenced in manuscripts of translated humorous stories and Polish jokes. (Editor's note in Sumtsov's publication, 1894d, p. 129).

'A Hutsul znakharka*', a photograph by H. Gasiorowski (circa 1920-1929).*

2.25. The Riddle–Tale

The Tsarivna loved riddle-tales and promised to marry any suitor who could tell her a riddle-tale she could not solve. However, if she solved it, the suitor would be executed.

One young man decided to try his luck. On the way, he shot blindly into a bush where something moved, killing a goat. Inside the goat, he found an unborn kid (foetus) and ate it. His horse then ate bread poisoned by the young man's mother and died. Four crows ate the horse meat and also died. The young man later found himself in the house of twelve robbers, who ate the four crows and died as well. Continuing his journey, he used the planks from his bed to cross a river.

When he reached the Tsarivna, he told her a riddle:

I was sprinting on a sprinter under the sun (i.e., on a horse);
I killed what I did not see (i.e., a goat);
I ate what was not born (i.e., a goat kid);
Four ate one, and twelve ate four;
I walked picking up "my trail" after myself.'

The Tsarivna, unable to guess the answer, sent her maids to the young man to learn it, but in vain. Since she could not solve the riddle, she married him.

_–^–_

40. Incomplete citation in the original. The reference likely pertains to A. Khomiakov's afterword in Kireyevskiy's song collection, specifically the song 'Would you like me, brothers, to tell you a tale', (1856, pp. 63–64).

Comments: Another Ukrainian version of this folk tale, from Halychyna region, is recorded under as no. 49 in Kolberg (1882–89, vol. 4, pp. 220–224), [see '1.49. Three Riddles' on page 70]. A similar Russian song was published in the *Works* by Khomiakov[40]. The riddle-tale is also related to the folk tale about 'Hurka, the Seven-Year-Old'.

2.26. Hurka, the Seven–Year–Old Girl

There were two brothers: one rich and the other poor. The rich brother had no children, while the poor brother had seven sons and one daughter [named Hurka]. The rich brother wanted to take the poor brother's only cow, so the matter went to trial before the *Pan*.

The *Pan* posed riddles: "What is the fastest thing in the world? What is the sweetest, and what is the fattest?" Hurka answered that a thought was the fastest, sleep was the sweetest, and the earth was the fattest. As a result, the rich brother's cows were awarded to the poor brother.

The *Pan* then presented Hurka with further trials. First, he sent her fifteen baked eggs and asked her to ensure chickens hatched from them. In response, Hurka sent him cooked millet *kasha* and asked him to sow it.

Next, the *Pan* ordered her to spin 100 ells of cloth from a handful of yarn. In return, Hurka sent him twigs and asked him to build a loom for her.

Finally, the *Pan* instructed Hurka to come to him riding but not riding, naked but wearing a *sorochka*, and with a gift but without one. Hurka wore a fishing net [and cleverly fulfilled the task].

The *Pan* married Hurka; he forbade her from resolving any disputes without him. However, during his absence, Hurka settled a quarrel between two peasants. Upon his return, the *Pan* demanded she take whatever was dearest to her and return to her father. Hurka intoxicated her husband, took him to her father's home as her most precious possession, and the couple reconciled.

_–^–_

Comments:Versions of this folk tale about the Wise Maiden have been referenced earlier in the discussions of the Halychyna-Rus folk tales '1.50 & 1.51. The Wise Maiden' on page 70 & '1.76. A Fairy Tale about a Clever Furrier' on page 91.

The literature on the subject is extensive, with the most comprehensive references listed in Child (1882–98, vol. 1, no. 2) [...].

2.27. How the Peasant Traded his Oxen

A peasant had a good wife and owned a pair of oxen. He traded his oxen for a cart, then the cart for a goat, the goat for a goose, the goose for a duck, the duck for a purse, and finally, when he needed to cross a river but lacked money, he gave his purse to the ferry drivers.

Along the way, he met some *chumaky*, who laughed at him upon hearing his story and predicted that his wife would thrash him for his foolish trades. The peasant made a bet with them: if his wife praised him instead, they would give him a pair of oxen and a cart full of salt. Two *chumaky* accompanied him home, and to their astonishment, they heard the wife praise her husband for his trades and thank God that he had returned alive and well.

_^_

Comments: Folk tales featuring the motif of trading objects for increasingly inferior items are found in many collections of folk tales, such as:

Ukrainian:

Chubynsky (1872–78, vol. 2, p. 97);
Drahomanov (1876, p. 360); and
Yastrebov (1894, pp. 176–178);

Belarusian:

Romanov (1887); and
Manzhura (1890, pp. 87–88).

French and other Western European: Cosquin (1886, vol. 1, pp. 155–157, no. 13).

'Chumak on the road; Farmer from the vicinity of Uman' by Jan Nepomucen Lewicki (1841).

'A Rus young man from Petranka village, Stryi county and a highlander from Pasichna village, Stanislaviv county, eastern Halychyna', (Holovatsky 1878, vol. 2, p. 1).

2.28. About the Foolish People in this World

A foolish maiden was crying because she imagined that when she was wedded and had a child, a chisel from the *pich* might fall on his head and kill him. When her mother and then her father heard this, they were saddened too.

Their son, angry with them, went into the world in search of even more foolish people. He came to a village where people were trying to pull a cow into the church because it had been bequeathed by a woman to the church. He advised them to sell the cow and donate the money to the church.

In another village, he saw a woman beating a hen for hatching fifteen chicks but not feeding them milk. He put the chicks under the hen and continued his journey. Finally, he reached a third village, where people were carrying light in sacks into a newly built church. He made windows in the walls to let the light in and was elected their priest. He ordered his parishioners to come to the church every time the bell tolled; otherwise, he threatened to take away their oxen.

One day, in the church, an ember from a censer fell inside the priest's boot; and he began to shake and stomp his foot, and all the parishioners copied him.

The villagers saw a sickle in the field, left by the priest, and mistook it for a beast. They began to beat the sickle with sticks; the sickle bounced back and cut off one man's head. The villagers thought it was a snake and ran to tell the priest. The priest mounted his horse and dragged the sickle with a rope. It looked as if the sickle was chasing after him, and thus he left the villagers behind.

Later, the priest met a woman who wanted to baptise her piglets. He tricked her by taking her horse and pretending to take the piglets to the church to be baptised. Her husband caught up with him, but the priest stuck the horse's tail into the ground and hid himself and the horse further ahead. The husband thought that the horse had gone into the ground and returned home.

The son returned home, realising that there were even more foolish people in the world than his parents and sister.

—^—

Comments: Tales about foolish peoples have long been very popular. In ancient Greece, motifs of foolishness were associated with the name of the Abderites, and in ancient Rus [Kyivan Rus], according to the allusions in some chronicles, with the Pechenegs [...].

The literature on the subject is extensive but disorganised. The motifs have been neither collected nor examined, except for the one about jumping into flowering buckwheat, as well as the sea, which has been discussed in Ivan Franko's article in *Wisla* (1892), and its addendum (1893)[40].

Tales about foolish people are found in:

> Shapkarev (1892–94, vol. 8, pp. 26–28, nos. 17 & 18; & pp. 65–72, nos. 54–56);
> Rudchenko (1869–70);
> Kolberg (1882–89, vol. 4, pp. 235–237), [here see '1.57. Three Brothers' on page 74];
> Ciszewski (1894, p. 221, nos. 169–170 & pp. 238–239, no. 188); and
> Veckenstedt (1880, p. 100).

40. The citation in the original is ambiguous, as there are several articles by Ivan Franko in the journal.

Dmytro Yavornytsky also published a related fable, 'Fable about Sniffers' (1889), among others.

'A church in Subotiv village, near Chyhyryn town, Kyiv province, founded by Hetman Khmelnytskyi' de la Flise (1854).

2.29. About the Wise Simpleton

There were three brothers: two were smart, and the third was a simpleton. All of them went to an old man for fire. (The old man was as short as a cork, and his beard was two fathoms long).

The old man demanded that they tell him a folk tale, a tale, and a tall tale. The two older brothers failed to tell the tales, and the old man tore a strip of skin from each of them, from head to toe.

The third brother, the Simpleton, made a deal with the old man: if the old man said to him, 'You are lying', the simpleton would remove a strip of the old man's skin from head to toe and rub him with coarse barley.

The simpleton told a nonsense verse about a bumblebee fighting a bear, a mare being torn in half while jumping across a river, and a horse-rider joining both halves of the mare with a stake. He also told of a willow growing from the stake and reaching the sky, and about the horse-rider climbing it to the sky, and so on.

The old man said, 'You're lying', and the simpleton took some of his fire, and cut a strip of the old man's skin from head to toe.

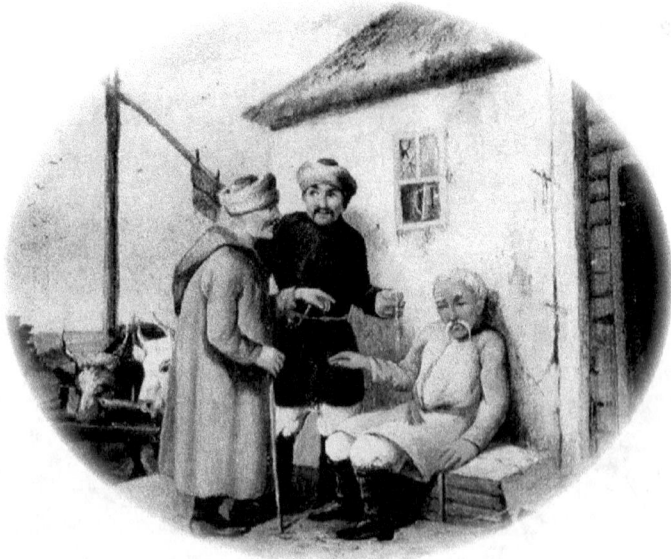

'Chumaky by a korchma' artist unknown (1840s), housed in Chernihiv Art Museum.

'Ukrainians' by V. Makovsky, published in Niva (1885, no. 16, p. 373).

2.30. How the Son and Father Managed on Their Own: a Nonsense Verse

The father and son were ploughing in a tavern under a bench. The son liked starlings and climbed into the hollow of a tree, where he freed himself by chopping an opening out with an axe. The axe produced small axes. They placed duck eggs under a pig, and lambs hatched out of them, and so on.

_^_

Comments: This folk tale, along with the previous one, '2.29. About the Wise Simpleton' on page 144, are nonsense verses or tall tales ['нісенітниця'; 'nisenitnytsia']. The term 'nisenitnytsia' is derived from the words 'ni te ni se' [Engl., 'neither this nor that'], […] and refers to a string of nonsense tales.

An interesting fact is that such tales are found in the folklore of various cultures and share significant similarities. Nonsense verses are found both in the form of folk tales and in the form of songs, mainly children's songs. See, for example, Belarusian songs in Shein's collection (Shein 1874).

Frontispiece by J. G. Bach (Hahn 1864, vol. 2).

See also:
Manzhura (1890, p. 123);
Kolberg (1882–89, vol. 4, pp. 271–280, no. 73, [here, see '1.73. Koshalky-Opalky' on page 86]);
Chubynsky (1872–78, vol. 2), p. 676, no. 141, and, p. 677, no. 142);
Yastrebov (1894, p. 11 & 178–180, no. 35);
Lopatinskiy (1891, p. 93);
Semenov (1893b, p. 47);
Zakharov (1890, p. 70);
Ulanowska (1884, p. 299);
Dobrovolskiy (1891, p. 659, no. 7); and
Hahn (1864, vol. 1, pp. 242–243, no. 39 & pp. 313–314, no. 59).

2.31. Kyryk

Kyryk was a poor man. When his child died, the priest refused to wait until autumn to be paid [for the funeral ceremony]. Following the *Pan's* advice Kyryk decided to bury his child himself.

An old man revealed to Kyryk the location of a treasure buried nearby, and Kyryk unearthed a cauldron full of money. For a payment of 15 rubles and a lavish treat, the priest agreed to bury his child.

On the advice of his wife, the priest decided to coerce all of Kyryk's money. He donned a cowhide with horns and, pretending to be the *chort*, appeared under Kyryk's window. However, the cowhide and horns became affixed to the priest.

_^_

Comments: The tale is narrated in verse form. A similar version is found in Chubynsky 1872–78, vol. 2, pp. 105–108, no. 31. A special study of this folk tale-fable was published by K. G. in *Bulletin of Europe* (K. G. 1887).[41]

Panteleimon Kulish (1819–1897).

41. A concise essay by F. Kudrynsky, published in *Kievskaya Starina* (Kudrynsky 1894), includes the text of the ballad 'About Kyryk and the greedy priest'. This essay provoked M. Drahomanov's article (1894). Thus, in his reference to the *Notes on Southern Rus* (Kulish 1856–57), Drahomanov unsubstantially criticised F. Kudrynsky for omitting a mention of the ballad, which was supposedly contained in said, P. Kulish's *Notes*. (It is a known fact that censorship extracted the ballad from Kulish's work, accidentally leaving it only in a few copies).

Back in the 1880s, I personally collected several Ukrainian and Polish versions of this satirical piece, which served as reference material for my report for the Ethnography Department (e.g., *Proceedings of the Imperial Society of Naturalists, Anthropologists and Ethnographers*).

The late editor of *Kievskaya Starina*, Feofan Lebedyntsev, used that report for his article, which could not have appeared in print back then.

However, now we have access to his article as well as the texts at our disposal. Around the same time, in *Kievskaya Starina* O. I. [surname unknown] concisely re-told a similar Volyn legend referencing an 'official document' (O. I. 1887). (Note from the editor (Sumtsov 1894b).

2.32. About Ivan the Priest's Hireling

(Lukashevych, 1909, p. 100)

The Priest hired Ivan the Hireling on the condition that if Ivan caused the Priest to lose his temper, he would cut off the Priest's nose and receive a hundred rubles. First, Ivan slaughtered the Priest's oxen, but the Priest did not lose his temper. Then, he killed the Priest's dog, and later, his children. The Priest and his wife fled. Ivan hid in a sack, which the Priest carried on his back. In the yard, Ivan drowned the Priest's wife, and finally, the Priest lost his temper, thus suffering the punishment as per their agreement.

2.33. About the Priest's Hireling

Book cover of Sopilka: a Fairy Tale *(Hrinchenko 1914).*

This version of the previous tale is simpler and contains fewer motifs. A distinctive feature here is that the Hireling owns a *sopilka*, and when he plays it, everyone is compelled to dance.

_⌃_

Comments: Tales about the Priest and his labourer, a strongman, are popular in Russia and Western Europe. In some French and other Western European folk tales the Priest is sometimes replaced by other heros. A. Pushkin heard this tale from his nanny Arina Rodionovna and transformed it into verse, 'A tale about a priest; and his worker Balda'. I will include a detailed study of Pushkin's verse and its folk versions in my article, 'Sketches on A. Pushkin', in *Russkiy Filologicheskiy Vestnik* [cf. Sumtsov 1893c & Sumtsov 1894c], so I will not discuss this motif further here.

2.34. About Lesko the Fool

The wife sent her foolish husband to her parents to bring back some goodies. They gave him a lamb, but he gave it to the dogs. When he returned, his wife scolded him, explaining that the lamb was meant for cooking, and sent him back to her parents. This time, they gave him a kerchief, and he cooked the kerchief. Continuing to misunderstand his wife's instructions, the foolish husband put the puppy behind his belt, tied his sister-in-law to the barn, and brought the horse to the table at home.

_‑^‑_

Comments: A similar Bulgarian folk tale ['5. Глупав зеть'] is included in *The Collection of Folk Tales* (Stoikov 1891, p. 128), and a Ukrainian version can be found in Manzhura (1890, p. 80).

Numerous versions of this folk tale exist across Western Europe (see also, V. Zhukovskiy's adaptation of 'Kannitverstan'[42]). The motif of this tale, which belongs to the wide range of narratives about simpletons, hinges on the literal interpretation of words or their retrospective misapplication.

Ivan Manzhura (1851–1893), Ukrainian poet, ethnographer, journalist, lexicographer, translator from Russian and German; published his collection of folk tales in 1890.

42. 'Kannitverstan' – is a short story (1808) by German author Johann Peter Hebel.

'The Foolish Shepherd', (Manzhura 1890, p. 81).

2.35. About the Woman who Wanted to get Married

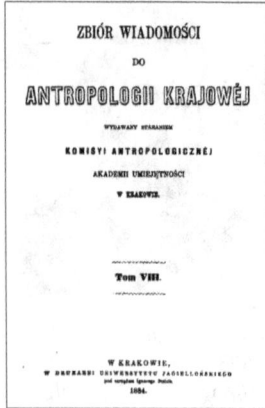

ZBIÓR WIADOMOŚCI

DO

ANTROPOLOGII KRAJOWĒJ

WYDAWANY STARANIEM

KOMISYI ANTROPOLOGICZNĒJ

AKADEMII UMIEJĘTNOŚCI

W KRAKOWIE.

Tom VIII.

W KRAKOWIE,
W DRUKARNI UNIWERSYTETU JAGIELLOŃSKIEGO
pod zarządem Ignacego Stelcla.
1884.

Nejman 1884c,

A son told his elderly mother about a decree requiring old men to marry young women and young men to marry old women, but only if the old woman climbed onto the roof, placed her leg behind her neck, and called out three times like a cuckoo. In his absence, the mother attempted the task, fell from the roof, and died.

_^_

Comments: Another Ukrainian version of this tale, 'How the Old Woman Married the Young Man', was recorded in the Kyiv province by Mrs Z D and published in *Zbior Wiadomosci*, (Neyman 1884c, p. 239). This version is more refined: here, it is not the son but a stranger who deceives the old woman. Furthermore, this version is significantly superior in literary quality.

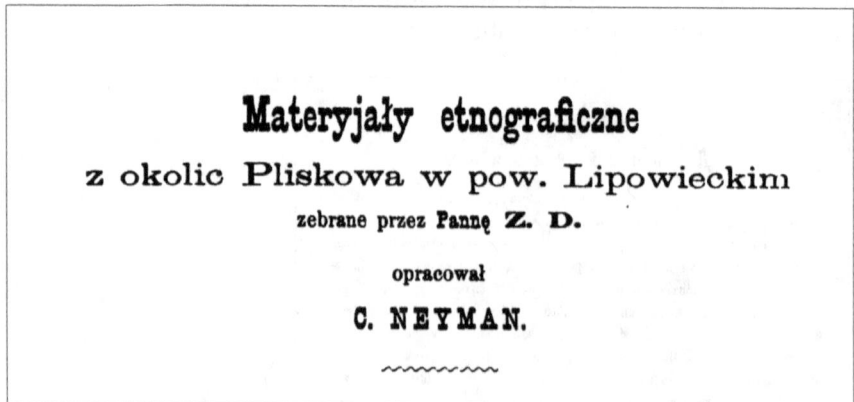

Materyjały etnograficzne

z okolic Pliskowa w pow. Lipowieckim

zebrane przez Pannę **Z. D.**

opracował

C. NEYMAN.

Nejman 1884c (p. 115)

2.36. Nonsense Verse No. 1

This nonsense verse is characterised by a series of repetitive events.

The magpie lost its tail and told the oak tree that if it explained how and why it had lost its tail, the oak tree would shed its leaves. The magpie shared its story, and the oak tree shed its leaves. When the sheep asked the oak tree why it had shed its leaves, they subsequently lost their wool.

Following this, the river turned bloody, the priest's maid fell with her buckets, the priest's wife danced around the house with a barrel upon learning why the maid had fallen, and the priest, in a fit of frustration, pulled out all his hair.

_^_

Here is another version:

Once there lived an old man and an old woman, and they had Hen the Riaba. She laid an egg, and the old man placed it on a shelf. A mouse scurried by and broke the egg. The old man and old woman despaired; the boar roared, the fence swayed, the oak tree broke its branches, the ox broke its horns, the maiden shattered her buckets, the priest's wife broke her barrel, and the priest demolished his church.'[43]

43. Hen the Riaba – is a famous Ukrainian tale. Riaba means speckled.

An illustration of an upset maiden breaking her buckets from 'The Old Man and the Old Woman' (Hrinchenko 1911).

'Lukash and Mavka' by Olena Sakhnovska (1929), illustration for Lesia Ukrainka's Lisova Pisnia *[Forest Song] (1911).*

2.37. Nonsense Verse No. 2

There once was a blade of grass. A sparrow flew up and said, 'Blade of grass, let me have a swing.' The blade of grass replied, 'I don't want to.'

The sparrow took its complaint about the blade of grass to an old goat; then he complained to a wolf about the goat, to the people about the wolf, to the Tatars about the people, to the fire about the Tatars, to the water about the fire, to the ox about the water, to the hammer about the ox, to the worms about the hammer, to the hens about the worms, to the hawk about the hens.

The sequence then reversed: the sparrow complained to the hens about the hawk, to the worms about the hens, and so forth, until finally, the blade of grass gave the sparrow a swing. Repetitions became increasingly frequent towards the end.

_^_

Comments: Nonsense verses like those found in 2.36 and 2.37 are often preserved as children's songs. Tales of this type are extensively represented in folk collections, such as:

Cosquin (1886, vol. 1, pp. 201–207, no. 18 & pp. 281–284, no. 29 & vol. 2, pp. 32–41, no. 34);

Chelchowski (1890–91, vol. 1, pp. 74 & 75);

Manzhura (1890, p. 5); and

Carnoy & Nicolaides (1889, pp. 184–186, no. 16).

Svitlana Soldatova's illustration for The Sparrow and the Bush *(Yakovenko & Soldatova 2018, pp. 6 & 7).*

The Worm became scared,
and was about to gnaw at the Axe's wooden handle,
the Axe was prepared to strike the Ox,
the Ox decided to drink all the Water,
the Water rushed to quench the Fire,

Svitlana Soldatova's illustration for The Sparrow and the Bush – the English translation of a version of '2.37. Nonsense Verse No. 2' (Yakovenko & Soldatova 2018, pp. 14 & 15).

the Fire was ready to burn the People's homes, the People made up their minds to kill the Wolf, the Wolf was about to eat the Goat and the Goat was very near to nibbling the Bush.

List of leading motifs in Moszynska's folk tales

The list is based on Mykola Sumtsov's original compilation of motifs from Moszynska's folk tales (Sumtsov 1894b, pp. 134–135). Entries marked with an asterisk (*) are retained from Sumtsov's original work, while the remaining entries are new additions derived from the author's commentaries.

Motif	Folk tale no.
Marko, the Rich*	no. 2.1.
Lucky simpleton	no. 2.2.
Magic objects (a table, ram, and stick beat-by-itself)*	no. 2.3.
Child abduction for cannibalism	no. 2.4.
Pesyholovtsi	no. 2.4.
Journey to the otherworld (Descent to the underworld; Tsardom of underworld)	no. 2.4.
Fate and luck (Taming *Dolia* [Fate])*	no. 2.5.
Insidious wife (mother)*	no. 2.5.
Prophetic election (Divine election of a *tsar*)*	no. 2.5.
Grateful animals*	no. 2.6.
Loss of the ring*	no. 2.6.
Miraculous conception	no. 2.7.

Motif	Folk tale no.
*Pokotyhoroshko**	no. 2.7.
Brother, the Little Ram*	no. 2.8.
Malevolent stepmother*	no. 2.9.
*Suchych**	no. 2.10.
Throwing of the boot*	no. 2.10.
Token of distress	no. 2.10.
Malevolent livestock (i.e. Koza-Dereza or the malicious goat)	no. 2.11.
Prophetic *sopilka**	no. 2.12.
Journey to the otherworld (The soldier in hell and heaven)*	no. 2.13.
Death's subjugation	no. 2.13.
Hubristic king*	no. 2.14.
Supernatural deer as a divine being*	no. 2.14.
Origins of human nature	no. 2.15.
Demonic retribution and reward	no. 2.16.
Maiden and robbers	no. 2.17.
Dolia [Fate]*	no. 2.18.
Foolish and lazy wife	no. 2.19.
Taming the wicked wife*	no. 2.20.
Human outwits supernatural being in a wager (A wager with the *chort* over the division of cereals and root crops)*	no. 2.21.
Fraudulent healer (A male healer)*	no. 2.22.
Propasnytsia's [Fever's] subjugation*	no. 2.23.
Fraudulent healer (A female healer)*	no. 2.24.
Riddle-Tale*	nos. 2.25 & 2.26.
The wise maiden*	no. 2.26.
Diminishing trades*	no. 2.27.
Foolish people*	no. 2.28.

Motif	Folk tale no.
Wise simpleton	no. 2.29.
Nonsense verses*	nos. 2.29 & 2.30.
Avaricious cleric (Greedy priest)*	no. 2.31.
Strongman servant (The priest's strongman hireling)*	no. 2.32.
Strongman servant (The priest's strongman hireling)*	no. 2.33.
The simpleton, who misunderstands the meaning of words*	no. 2.34.
The old woman who wished to wed*	no. 2.35.
Animal tales of questions and complaints*	nos. 2.36 & 2.37.

Bibliography

Afanasiev, A 1865–69, *Poeticheskiye Vozzreniya Slavian na Prirodu* [Poetic Views of the Slavs on Nature], (in 3 vols.: 1865, 1868 & 1869), Soldatenkov, Moscow.

Antonovych, V & Drahomanov, M 1874-75, *Istoricheskie Pesni Malorusskogo Naroda* [Historical Songs of Ukrainian People], (in 2 vols.), Frits Publishing, Kyiv.

Antonovych, V 1877, *Koldovstvo: Dokumenty, Protsessy i Issledovanie* [Witchcraft: Documents, Court Proceedings and Research], V Kirshbaum Printing House, Saint Petersburg.

Avenarius, V 1876, *Kniga o Kyivskikh Bohatyriakh* [The Book of Kyivan Bohatyri], Stasiulevich Printing House, Saint Petersburg.

Bain, R N 1894, Cossack Fairy Tales and Folk-Tales, Lawrence and Bullen, London.

Barącz, S 1866, *Bajki, Fraszki, Podania, Przyslowa i Piesni na Rusi* [Fairy Tales, Epigrams, Legends, Proverbs and Songs in Rus], Druk Anny Wajdowiczowej, Lviv.

Barbazan, É 1756, *Fabliaux et contes des poetes françois des XII, XIII, XIV, & XVes siècles* [Fabliaux and Tales by French Poets of the 12th, 13th, 14th, and 15th Centuries], (in 3 vols.), Vincent, Paris.

Benfey, T 1857–59, *Panchatantra: Fünf Bücher indischer Fabeln, Märchen und Erzählungen* [Panchatantra: Five Books of Indian Fables, Fairy Tales and Stories], (in 2 vols.), Brockhaus, Leipzig.

Bezhanov, M 1894, 'Vartashenskie Evrei: Ocherk ikh byta, legendy i skazki' [Vartashen (Oghuz) Jews: article on their life, legends and fairy tales], *Sbornik Materialov dlia Opisaniya Kavkaza* [Collection of Materials for Description of the Caucasus], vol. XVIII, part 3, pp. 110–227.

Buslaev, F 1861, 'Pesni drevney Eddy o Zigurde i Muromskaya legenda' [Songs of the Poetic Edda about Zigurda and the Muromsky tale], *Istoricheskiye Ocherki Russkoy Narodnoy Slovesnosti i Iskusstva* [Historical Sketches on Russian Folk Literature and Art], (in 2 vols.), Kozhanchikov Publishing, Saint Petersburg.

Carnoy, E & Nicolaides, J 1889, *Traditions Populaires de l'Asie Mineure* [Popular Traditions of Asia Minor], Maisonneuve & Ch. Leclerc, Paris.

Chelchowski, S 1890-91, *Powieści i Opowiadania Ludowe z Okolic Przasnysza* [Folk Tales and Stories from the Vicinity of Przasnysz], (in 2 vols.), Biblioteka 'Wisła', (vols. 3 & 4), Warsaw.

Child, F 1882–98, *The English and Scottish Popular Ballads*, (in 5 vols.), Houghton, Mifflin and Company, Boston and New York.

Chubynsky, P 1872–78, *Trudy Etnografichesko-Statisticheskoy Ekspeditsii v Zapadno-Russkiy Kray* [Works of the Ethnographic-Statistical Expedition to the Western Rus Lands] (in 7 vols.), Maikov, Saint Petersburg.

Ciszewski, S 1894, *Krakowiacy: Monografia Etnograficzna* [Cracovians: Ethnographic Monograph], vol. 1, Krakow.

Cosquin, E 1886, *Contes Populaires de Lorraine* [Popular Tales of Lorraine], (in 2 vols.), Vieweg, Paris.

Dashkevych, M 1893, 'Vopros o literaturnom istochnike ukrainskoy opery I. P. Kotliarevskogo "Moskal-Charivnyk" ' [Discussion on literary source of I. P. Kotliarevsky's 'The Muscovite-Sorcerer', Ukrainian opera], *Kievskaya Starina* [Kyivan Antiquity], vol. 43, no. 12, pp. 451–482.

Dobrovolskiy, V. 1891, *Smolenskiy Etnograficheskiy Sbornik* [Smolensk Ethnographic Collection], (in 4 vols.; 1891–1903), Zapiski Imperatorskogo Russkogo Geograficheskogo Obshchestva [Notes of the Imperial Russian Geographical Society], vol. 1.

Drahomanov, M 1876, *Malorusskie Narodnye Predania i Rasskazy* [Ukrainian Folk Legends and Stories], Izdanie Yugo-Zapadnogo Otdela Imperatorskogo Russkogo Geograficheskogo Obshchestva [South-Western Division of Russian Imperial Geographical Society], Kyiv.

Drahomanov, M 1891, 'Slavyanskitye pryepravki na Edipovata istoriya' [Slavic adaptations of the Oedipus story], *Sbornik za Narodni Umotvoreniya* [The Collection of Folk Tales], vol. 5, pp. 267–310.

Drahomanov, M 1892, 'Zabyelyezhki verkhu slavyanskitye religiozni i ezicheski legendi' [Notes on Slavic religious and pagan legends], *Sbornik za Narodni Umotvoreniya* [The Collection of Folk Tales], vol. 7, pp. 245–310.

Drahomanov, M 1894, 'Protyvopopivska satyra i sektanty na Ukrayini' [Anti-priest satire and sectarians in Ukraine], *Zhytie i Slovo* [Life and Word], vol. 2, pp. 153–155.

Eivazov, P 1894, 'Aisorskie legendy i skazki' [Assyrian legends and tales], *Sbornik Materialov dlia Opisaniya Kavkaza* [Collection of Materials for Description of the Caucasus], vol. 18, part 3, pp. 59–109.

Gonzenbach, L 1870, *Sicilianische Märchen* [Sicilian Folk Tales], (in 2 vols.), W Engelmann, Leipzig.

Grabowski, B 1892, 'Podania o związkach między najbliższym rodzeństwem' [Stories about relations between siblings], *Wisła*, vol. 6.

Granstrem, E (trans.) 1881, *Kalevala: Finskiy Narodnyi Epos* [Kalevala: the Finnish Folk Epic], V. S. Balashev, Saint Petersburg.

Hahn, J G 1864, *Griechische und Albanesische Märchen* [Greek and Albanian Fairy Tales], (in 2 vols.), Engelmann, Leipzig.

Holovatsky, Y 1878, *Narodni Pisni Halytskoyi ta Uhorskoy Rusi* [Folk Songs of Galician and Hungarian Rus], (in 3 vols; vol. 3: in 2 parts), Moscow University Printing House, Moscow.

Hrinchenko, B 1911, *The Mitten & The Old Man and the Old Woman*, Ukrainskyi Uchytel [Ukrainian Teacher] Publishing, Kyiv.

Hrinchenko, B 1914, *Sopilka: Kazka* [Sopilka: a Fairy Tale], Bondarenko &

Kozlovskyi Printing House, Kyiv.

Ivanov, P 1890–1893, 'Iz oblasti malorusskikh narodnykh legend' [From the area of Ukrainian folk legends], *Etnograficheskoe Obozrenie* [Ethnographic Review], 1890, book 5, pp. 142–156; 1890, book 7, pp. 71–94; 1891, book 9, pp. 110–132; 1892, books 13–14, pp. 65–97; 1893, book 17, pp. 70–91 & 1893, book 18, pp. 85–120.

K, G 1887, 'Dva malorossiyskikh "fablo", i ikh istochniki. Iz istorii vseobshchey sravnitelnoy literatury' [Two Ukrainian 'fablo' and their sources. From the history of general comparative literature], *Vestnik Yevropy* [The Bulletin of Europe], vol. 4, book 7, pp. 323–352.

Kallash, V 1890, 'Melkiye etnograficheskiye zametki: Chobotko ili Chobotok' [Brief ethnographic notes: Chobotko or Chobotok] *Etnograficheskoe Obozrenie* [Ethnographic Review], vol. 5, no. 2, pp. 250–258.

Karadžić, V 1845, *Srpske Narodne Pjecme* [Serbian Folk Songs], Armenian Monastery Printing House, Vienna.

Karadžić, V 1870, *Srpske Narodne Pripovijetke* [Serbian Folk Tales], Ana udovica V.S. Karadžića, Vienna.

Karlowicz, J 1887, 'Podania i baiki ludowe zabrane na Litwie' [Folk tales and legends recorded in Lithuania], *Zbiór Wiadomości do Antropologii Krajowej* [A Collection of Materials on National Anthropology], vol. 11, part 3, pp. 229–293.

Karlowicz, J 1888, 'Podania i baiki ludowe zabrane na Litwie' [Folk tales and legends recorded in Lithuania], *Zbiór Wiadomości do Antropologii Krajowej* [A Collection of Materials on National Anthropology], vol. 12, part 3, pp. 1–59.

Kazbek, N 1890, 'Tatarskie skazki, zapisannye v Geokchayskom uezde, Bakinskoy gubernii [Tatar tales, recorded in the Geokchay district, Baku governorate], *Sbornik Materialov dlia Opisaniya Kavkaza* [Collection of Materials for Description of the Caucasus], vol. 9, pp. 75–102.

Khalanskiy, M 1893–96, *Yuzhnoslavyanskiye Skazaniya o Kraleviche Marke v Svyazi s Proizvedeniyami Russkogo Bylevogo Eposa* [South Slavic Legends about King Mark in relation to the Works of the Russian Byl-Epic Poetry], (in 4 vols.), Tipografia Varshavskogo Uchebnogo Okruga [Warsaw Educational District Printing House], Warsaw.

Khudiakov, I 1860–62, *Velikorusskie Skazki* [Russian Fairy Tales], (in 3 vols.), Grachov Printing House (vols. 1 & 2), Military Printing House (vol. 3), Saint Petersburg.

Kikot, V 1893, 'Skazki, predrazsudki, poslovitsy, pogovorki i zagadki zapisannye v stanitse Uma-khan-Yurtovskoy' [Fairy tales, superstitions, sayings and proverbs recorded in Umakhan-Yurtovskaya stanytsia], *Sbornik Materialov dlia Opisaniya Kavkaza* [Collection of Materials for Description of the Caucasus], vol. 15, part 2, pp. 179–192.

Kireyevskiy, P 1856, 'Russkiye narodnyye pesni' [Russian folk songs] *Russkaya Beseda* [Russian Conversation], book 1, pp. 44–64.

Kolberg, O 1857, Pieśni ludu polskiego, Nakladem Wydawcy, Warsaw.

Kolberg, O 1857–90, *Lud. Jego Zwyczaje, Sposób, Życia, Mowa, Podania, Przysłowia, Obrzędy, Gusła, Zabawy, Pieśni, Muzyka i Tańce* [People: their Customs, Way of Life, Language, Legends, Proverbs, Rites, Witchcraft, Games, Songs, Music, and Dances], (in 33 vols.), The Jagiellonian University Printing House, Kraków.

Kolberg, O 1882–89, *Pokucie: Obraz Etnograficzny* [Pokuttia: Ethnographic Portrait] (in 4 vols.: vols. 29–33 in Kolberg O, 1857–90, Lud: Jego Zwyczaje, Sposób, Życia, Mowa, Podania, Przysłowia, Obrzędy, Gusła, Zabawy, Pieśni, Muzyka i Tańce [People: their Customs, Way of Life, Language, Legends, Proverbs, Rites, Witchcraft, Games, Songs, Music, and Dances], (in 33 vols.), The Jagiellonian University Printing House, Kraków.

Koropchevskiy, D (ed. & trans.) 1874, *Basni i Skazki Dikikh Narodov* [Fables and Folk Tales of Wild Peoples], (Translation of Bleek, W 1864, 'Reynard the Fox in South Africa'; and Callaway, H 1868, 'Nursery Tales, Traditions and Histories of the Zulus'), (in 2 vols.), V Demakov, Saint Petersburg.

Kosach, L & Kvitka, K 1903, *Detskiye Igry, Pesni i Skazki Kovelskogo, Lutskogo i Novograd-Volynskogo Uyezdov Volynskoy Guberniyi* [Children's Games, Songs and Tales of the Kovel, Lutsk and Novograd-Volynsky Counties of the Volyn Province],

Chokolov Printing House, Kyiv.

Kosinski, W 1881, 'Materyjaly do etnografii Gorali Bieskidowych' [Materials on the ethnography of the Beskid Gorals], *Zbiór Wiadomości do Antropologii Krajowej* [A Collection of Materials on National Anthropology], vol. 5, pp. 187–265.

Kremnitz, M 1882, *Rumänische Märchen* [Romanian Fairy Tales], Verlag von Wilhelm Friedrich, Leipzig.

Kriukov, B 1929, *Koza-Dereza* [The Goat-Dereza], Ukrainian State Publishing, Kyiv.

Kudrynsky, F 1894, 'O Kyryke i zhadnom pope' [About Kyryk and greedy priest], *Kievskaya Starina* [Kyivan Antiquity], vol. 44, no. 3, pp. 543–548.

Kulchytska, O 1959, *Narodnyi Odiah Zakhidnykh oblastei Ukrainy* [Folk Clothing of the Western Regions of the Ukrainian SSR], Publishing House of the Academy of Sciences of the Ukrainian SSR, Kyiv.

Kulish, P 1856–57, *Zapiski o Yuzhnoy Rusi* [Notes on Southern Rus], (in 2 vols), P Kulish, Saint Petersburg.

Lominadze, S 1894, 'Mingrelskie skazki', [Mingrelian folk tales], *Sbornik Materialov dlia Opisaniya Kavkaza* [Collection of Materials for Description of the Caucasus], vol. 18, pp. 27–48.

Lopatinskiy, L 1891, 'Kabardinskie predaniya, skazaniya i skazki, zapisannye po-russki' [Kabardin legends, myths and fairy tales recorded in Russian], *Sbornik Materialov dlia Opisaniya Kavkaza* [Collection of Materials for Description of the Caucasus], vol. 12, pp. 1–144.

Lukashevych, K (tr.) 1909, *Malorossiyskiye Skazki dlia Detey* [Ukrainian Folk Tales for Children], I D Sytin Publishing, Moscow.

Luzel, F-M 1881, *Légendes chrétiennes de la Basse-Bretagne* [Christian Legends of Lower Brittany], (in 3 vols.), Maisonneuveh, Paris.

Maksimilyanov, E 1893, 'Skazka "Vor" zapisannaya v slobode Vozdvizhenskoy, Hroznenskogo okruha' ['The Thief', a fairy tale recorded in Vozdvizhenska sloboda, Hroznenskiy region], *Sbornik Materialov dlia Opisaniya Kavkaza* [Collection of Materials for Description of the Caucasus], vol. 15, part 2, pp. 193–195.

Maliarenko, H 1750s, *Kuzhbushok Album: Drawings and Sketches by Students of the Kyiv Pechersk Lavra Monastery Workshop*, no. 14, Kyiv Pechersk Lavra, Kyiv.

Manzhura, I 1890, *Skazki, Poslovitsy i t. p., Zapisannye v Yekaterinoslavskoy i Kharkovskoy gubernii* [Fairy Tales, Proverbs, etc., Recorded in the Yekaterynoslav and Kharkiv Provinces], Sbornik Kharkovskogo Istoriko-Filologicheskogo Obshchestva [Collection of the Kharkiv Historical and Philological Society], Kharkiv.

Margolin, P (tr.) 1880, 'Skazaniya o Solomone perevel s yevreyskogo P. V. Margolin' [The Legends about Solomon, translated from the Hebrew by P. V. Margolin], *Pamiatniki Drevney Pismennosti* [Treasures to the Ancient Writings], issue 3, pp. 1–41.

Mashurko, M 1894, 'Iz oblasti narodnoy fantazii i byta Tiffliyskoy i Kutaisskoy gubernii', [From the Realm of Folk Fantasy and Everyday Life of the Tiflis and Kutaisi Governorates], *Sbornik Materialov dlia Opisaniya Kavkaza* [Collection of Materials for Description of the Caucasus], vol. 18, pp. 228–410.

Maspero, G 1889, *Les Contes Populaires de l'Égypte Ancienne* [Popular Tales of Ancient Egypt], J Maisonneuve, Paris.

Meon, M 1823, *Nouveau Recueil de Fabliaux et Contes Inédits, des Poètes Français des XIIe, XIIIe, XIVe et XVe Siècles* [New Collection of Unpublished Fabliaux and Tales by French Poets of the 12th, 13th, 14th, and 15th Centuries], (in 2 vols.), Chasseriau, Paris.

Milkovytskyi, A (ill) 1975, *Kotyhoroshko*: Ukrainian Folk Tales, Veselka Children's Book Publishing, Kyiv.

Miller, V 1893, 'Otgoloski apokrifov v kavkazkikh narodnykh skazaniyakh' [Echoes of the apocrypha in the Caucasian folk legends], *Zhurnal Ministerstva Narodnogo Prosveshcheniya* [Journal of the Ministry of Public Education], July, issue 288, pp. 94–103.

Minaev, I 1876, *Indiyskie Skazki i Legendy, Sobrannye v Kamaone v 1875 Godu* [Indian Folk Tales and Legends, Recorded in Kumaon in 1875], Demakov, Saint Petersburg.

Mizroev, A 1892, 'Armianskie skazki, predaniya i legendy: Lisitsa' [Armenian folk tales, stories and legends: Fox], *Sbornik Materialov dlia Opisaniya Kavkaza* [Collection of Materials for Description of the Caucasus], vol. 13, part 2, pp. 130–140.

Mo[szk]ow, W 1891, 'Bajka-zagadka o zabitym kochanku' [Fairy tale and puzzle about a killed lover], *Wisła*, vol. 5, part 1, pp. 138–153.

Mochulskiy, V 1887, *Istoriko-Literaturnyi Analiz Stikha o Golubinoy Knige* [Historical and Literary Analysis of the Verse about the Book of the Dove], M Zemkevich Printing House, Warsaw.

Moszynska, J 1885, 'Bajki i zagadki ludu Ukrainskiego' [Fairy Tales and Riddles of the Ukrainian People], *Zbiór Wiadomości do Antropologii Krajowej* [A Collection of Materials for National Anthropology], vol. 9.

Nasir-Sultanov, B 1892, 'Tatarskie skazki i predania zapisanye v Elisavetpolskoy gubernii: Kharkhali' [The Tatar fairy tales and legends recorded in Elisavetpolsk province: Malik-Mamed], *Sbornik Materialov dlia Opisaniya Kavkaza* [Collection of Materials for Description of the Caucasus], vol. 13, part 2, pp. 305–308.

Nejman, C 1884a, 'Pokucie: Etnograficheskiy etiud, Oskar Kolberg, s politipazhami po risunkam T. Rybkovskogo. Krakow: tom 1 (1882) and tom 2 (1883)' [Pokuttia: Ethnographic study, compiled by Oskar Kolberg, with images based on drawings by T. Rybkovskiy. Krakow: volume 1 (1882) and volume 2 (1883)], *Kievskaya Starina* [Kyivan Antiquity], vol. 8, no. 3, pp. 482–487.

Nejman, C 1884b, 'Kolberg Oskar: Pokucie, etnograficheskiy etiud, tom 2, Krakow, 1883' [Kolberg Oskar: Pokuttia, Ethnographic study, volume 2, Krakow, 1883], *Kievskaya Starina* [Kyivan Antiquity], vol. 8, no. 5, pp. 126–130.

Nejman, C 1884c, 'Materiały etnograficzne z okolic Pliskowa w powiecie Lipowieckim. Zebrane przez pannę Z. D.' [Ethnographic materials from the area around Pliskow in the Lipowiecki district. Collected by Miss Z. D.], *Zbiór Wiadomości do*

Antropologii Krajowej [A Collection of Materials on National Anthropology], vol. 8, pp. 115–246.

O, I 1887, 'Volynskaya byvalshchina' [A Volyn legend], *Kievskaya Starina* [Kyivan Antiquity], vol. 19, no. 10, pp. 384–387.

Ortoli, J B F 1883, 'Les contes populaires de l'ile de Corse' [Popular tales from the island of Corsica], *Les Littératures Populaires de Toutes Les Nations* [Folk Literatures of All Nations], vol. 16, Paris, Maisonneuve.

Osipov, H 1892, 'Armianskie skazki, predaniya i legendy: Neblagodarnost' [Armenian folk tales, stories and legends: Ingratitude], *Sbornik Materialov dlia Opisaniya Kavkaza* [Collection of Materials for Description of the Caucasus], vol. 13, part 2, pp. 82–85.

Pamukchiev, I 1891, 'Prikazki iz cheliadniya i obshchestven zhivot... ot Troyan' [Tales on family and public life... from Troyan town], *Sbornik za Narodni Umotvoreniya* [The Collection of Folk Tales], vol. 6, pp. 125–126.

Pavlovych, H (ill.) 1921, *Koza-Dereza: Kazka* [Koza-Dereza: Fairy Tale], Adriy's Printing House, Vienna.

Piatirublev, B 1893, 'Skazki zapisannye v stanitse Naurskoy' [Fairy tales recorded in Naurskaya stanytsia] *Sbornik Materialov dlia Opisaniya Kavkaza* [Collection of Materials for Description of the Caucasus], vol. 15, part 2, pp. 147–178.

Podbereski, A 1880, 'Materialy do demonologii ludu Ukrainkiego' [Materials on demonology of the Ukrainian people], *Zbiór Wiadomości do Antropologii Krajowej* [A Collection of Materials on National Anthropology], vol. 4, part 3, pp. 3–82.

Porfiryev, I 1890, *Apokrificheskiye Skazaniya o Novozavetnykh Litsakh i Sobytiyakh po Rukopisiam Solovetskoy Biblioteki* [Apocryphal Legends about New Testament Personalities and Events Based on Manuscripts from the Solovki Library], Imperial Academy of Sciences, Saint Petersburg.

Potanin, G 1881–83, *Ocherki Severo-Zapadnoy Mongolii* [Essays on Northwest Mongolia], (in 4 issues: issues 1 & 3 Tipografiya V Bezobrazova [V Bezobrazov Printing House] & issues 2 & 4, Tipografiya V Kirshbaum [V Kirshbaum Printing House], Saint Petersburg.

Potebnia, O 1865, *O Mificheskom Znachenii Nekotorykh Poveriy i Obriadov* [About the Mythical Meaning of Some Beliefs and Rituals], Moscow University Press, Moscow.

Potebnia, O 1881, *K Istorii Zvukov Russkogo Yazyka* [On the History of the Sounds of the Russian Language], Tipografiya M Zemkevicha & V Noakovskogo [M Zemkevich & V Noakovsky Printing House], Warsaw.

Pypin, A 1857, *Ocherk Literaturnoy Istorii Starinnykh Povestey i Skazok Russkikh* [Essay on the Literary History of Old Russian Stories and Fairy Tales], Tipografiya Imperatorskoy Akademiyi Nauk [Imperial Academy of Sciences Printing House], Saint Petersburg.

Pypin, A 1890–92, *Istoriya Russkoy Etnografiyi* [History of Russian Ethnography], (in 4 vols.), Tipografiya MM Stasiulevicha [MM Stasiulevich Printing House], Saint Petersburg.

Ryabushkin, A (il.) 1895, *Russkiye Bylinnye Bohatyri* [Rus Epic Bohatyri], Hermann Hoppe Publishing, Saint Petersburg.

Riabykh, N 1893, 'Selo Spaskoe, Stavropolskoy gubernii, Novogrigoryevskogo uezda' [Spaskoe village, Stavropol province, Novogrigoryevskiy county] *Sbornik Materialov dlia Opisaniya Kavkaza* [Collection of Materials for Description of the Caucasus], vol. 16, part 1, pp. 278–307.

Romanov, E 1887, *Belorusskiy Sbornik. Vypusk Tretiy: Skazki* [Belarusian Collection. The Third Issue: Folk Tales], GA Malkin, Vitebsk.

Rudchenko, I 1869–70, *Narodnyia Yuzshnorusskiya Skazki* [Southern Rus Folk Tales], (in 2 vols.), V tipohrafii Fedorova [Fedorov Printing House], Kyiv.

Rudchenko, I 1920a, *Ukrainski Narodni Kazky: Popovych Yasat; Pravda ta Nepravda* [Ukrainian Folk Tales: Yasat, the Priest's Son; Truth and Falsehood], Ukrainian Publishing, Katerynoslav.

Rudchenko, I 1920b, *Ukrainski Narodni Kazky: Hordyi tsar; Pro Tsarenka Ivana ta Chortovu Dochku* [Ukrainian Folk Tales: The Arrogant Tsar; About Tsarenko Ivan and the Chort's Daughter], Ukrainian Publishing, Katerynoslav.

Rudchenko, I 1920c, *Ukrayinski Narodni Kazky: Rys-Maty; Brat i Sestra v Lisi*

[Ukrainian Folk Tales: Lynx-Mother; Brother and Sister in the Forest], Ukrainian Publishing, Katerynoslav.

Rudchenko, I 1920d, *Ukrayinski Narodni Kazky: Ubohyi ta Bahatyi i Divka–Chornavka; Bezshchasnyi Danylo ta Rozumna Zhinka* [Ukrainian Folk Tales: The Poor Man, the Rich Man, and the Dark-Haired Girl; Unfortunate Danylo and his Wise Wife], Ukrainian Publishing, Katerynoslav.

Sadovnikov, D 1884, 'Skazki i predaniya Samarskogo kraya' [Folk tales and legends of Samara region] *Zapiski Imperatorskogo Russkogo Geograficheskogo Obshchestva po Otdeleniyu Etnografii* [Notes of Ethnography Division, Imperial Russian Geographical Society], vol. 12.

Sanakoev, I 1890, ' "Skazka o Zmee-Tsare" soobshchil uchitel Baraletskoy selskoy shkoly', ["The Tale of the Zmey-Tsar" aas reported by a teacher from the Baraletsk Rural School], *Sbornik Materialov dlia Opisaniya Kavkaza* [Collection of Materials for Description of the Caucasus], vol. 9, pp. 182–183.

Sapundzhiev, I 1891, 'Prikazki za zli dukhove i dr.' [Tales about evil spirits etc.], *Sbornik za Narodni Umotvoreniya* [Collection of Folk Tales], vol. 6, pp. 110–111.

Sarksiants, M 1892, 'Tatarskie skazki i predania zapisanye v Elisavetpolskoy gubernii: Malik-Mamed' [The Tatar fairy tales and legends recorded in Elisavetpolsk province: Malik-Mamed], *Sbornik Materialov dlia Opisaniya Kavkaza* [Collection of Materials for Description of the Caucasus], vol. 13, part 2, pp. 308–318 & 321.

Schiefner, M 1869, 'Ueber einige morgenlændische Fassungen der Rampsinitsage' [About some Moroccan versions of the Rampsinite saga'], *Bulletin de l'Acad. Imp. de Sciences* [Imperial Academy of Sciences], vol. 6, March, p. 161.

Schleicher, A 1857, *Litauische Märchen, Sprichworte, Rätsel und Lieder* [Lithuanian Fairy Tales, Proverbs, Riddles and Songs], H Boehlau, Weimar.

Schonwerth, F 1858, *Aus der Oberpfalz: Sitten und Sagen* [From the Upper Palatinate: Customs and Legends], (in 3 vols.: 1857, 1858 & 1859), M Rieger Publishing, Augsburg, vol. 2.

Schott, A & A 1845, *Walachische Marchen* [Wallachian Fairy Tales], JG Cottascherr Verlag, Stuttgart & Tubingen.

Semenov, P 1893a, 'Neskolko stranichek iz zhizni kazakov st. Sleptsovskoy, Sunzhenkogo otdela, Terskoy oblasti' [Several pages from the lives of kozaky of Steptsovskaya stanytsia, Sunzha district, Terskaya (Terek) region] *Sbornik Materialov dlia Opisaniya Kavkaza* [Collection of Materials for Description of the Caucasus], vol. 16, part 1, pp. 162–210.

Semenov, P 1893b, 'Skazki zapisannye v stanitse Sleptsovskoy' [Fairy tales recorded in Steptsovskaya stanytsia] *Sbornik Materialov dlia Opisaniya Kavkaza* [Collection of Materials for Description of the Caucasus], vol. 15, part 2, pp. 1–146.

Shapkarev, K 1892, 'Bulgarski prikaski i vyerovaniya s pribavlenie na nyekolko Makedonovlashki i Albanski' [Bulgarian proverbs and beliefs with the addition of several Macedonian and Albanian ones] (in 2 parts), *Sbornik za Narodni Umotvoreniya* [The Collection of Folk Tales], (vols. 8 & 9), Liberalny Klub, Sofia.

Shein, P 1874, *Belorusskie Narodnye Pesni* [Belarusian Folk Songs], Maikov, Saint Petersburg.

Shepelevich, L 1891–92, *Etiydy o Dante* [Etudes on Dante], (in 2 vols.), A Darre, Kharkiv.

Singer, S von 1892, 'Sagengeschichtliche Parallelen aus dem babylonischen Talmud' [Legendary parallels from the Babylonian Talmud], *Zeitschrift des Vereins fur Volkskunde* [The Folklore Association Journal], pp. 293–301.

Stoikov, D 1891, 'Prikazki iz cheliadniya i obshtestvenu zhivotu ot Sofiiysko' [Tales from the family and public life: from Sofia], *Sbornik za Narodni Umotvoreniya* [The Collection of Folk Tales], vol. 6, pp. 126–129.

Sukhomlynov, M 1862, 'O predaníyakh v drevney russkoy letopisi' [About legends in the ancient Rus chronicles], *Osnova* [Foundation], pp. 51–71.

Sumtsov, M 1889, 'Kulturnye perezhivaniya: olen v proizvedeniyakh narodnoy slovesnosti i iskusstve' [Cultural experiences: deer in works of folk literature and art], *Kievskaya Starina* [Kyivan Antiquity], parts 1–4, vol. 24, no. 1, pp. 65–74.

Sumtsov, M 1890, 'Otgoloski khristianskikh predaniy v mongolskikh skazkakh' [Echoes of Christian legends in Mongolian Tales], *Etnograficheskoe Obozrenie* [Ethnographic Review], no. 3, pp. 1–20.

Sumtsov, M 1891, 'Mysha v narodnoy slovesnosti (s dopolneniyami k statye o vorone)' [Mouse in folklore (a supplement to the article about raven)], *Etnograficheskoe Obozrenie* [Ethnographic Review], vol. 8, no. 1, pp. 49–94.

Sumtsov, M 1892, 'Pesni o goste Terentii i rodstvennya im skazki' [Songs about Terentiy the guest and akin folk tales], *Etnograficheskoe Obozrenie* [Ethnographic Review], no. 1, pp. 106–120.

Sumtsov, M 1893a, 'H. Kvitka kak etnograf' [H. Kvitka as ethnographer], *Kievskaya Starina* [Kyivan Antiquity], vol. 42, no. 8, pp. 190–214.

Sumtsov, M 1893b, 'Muzh na svadbe svoey zheny' [Husband at a wedding of his wife], *Etnograficheskoe Obozrenie* [Ethnographic Review], no. 4, pp. 1–25.

Sumtsov, M 1893c, 'Etiudy ob A. S. Pushkine' [Sketches on A. Pushkin], Russkiy *Filologicheskiy Vestnik* [Russian Philological Bulletin], no. 29, part 1, pp. 148–163 [Prorok] & part 2, pp. 353–382; no. 30, part 3, pp. 158-173 & part 4, pp. 328–339.

Sumtsov, M 1894a, 'Etiudy ob A. S. Pushkine' [Sketches on A. Pushkin] Russkiy *Filologicheskiy Vestnik* [Russian Philological Bulletin], no. 31, parts 1–2, pp. 269–304; no. 32, part 3, pp. 45–76, part 4, pp. 155–174.

Sumtsov, M 1894b, *Malorusskiya Skazki po Sbornikam Kolberga i Moshinskoy* [Ukrainian Folk Tales in Collections of Kolberg and Moszynska], AA Levenson, Moscow.

Sumtsov, M 1894c, 'Skazki i legendy o Marke Bagatom' [Folk tales and legends about Marko the Rich], *Etnograficheskoe Obozrenie* [Ethnographic Review], vol. 20, no. 1, pp. 9–29.

Sumtsov, M 1894d, 'Dopolneniya i popravki k statye o Marke Bagatom' [Additions and amendments to the article about Marko the Rich], *Etnograficheskoe Obozrenie* [Ethnographic Review], vol. 21, no. 2, pp. 176–177.

Sumtsov, M 1894e, *Razbor Etnograficheskikh Trudov Romanova* [Analysis

of Ethnographic Works of Romanov], Tipografiya Imperatorskoy Akademiyi Nauk [Imperial Academy of Sciences
Printing House], Saint Petersburg.

Sumtsov, M ors 2019, *The Story of Pysanka: a Collection of Articles on
Ukrainian Easter Eggs*, Sova Books, Sydney.

Teptsov, Y 1894, 'Iz byta i verovaniy mingreltsev' [From the everyday
life and beliefs of the Mingrelians], *Sbornik Materialov dlia
Opisaniya Kavkaza* [Collection of Materials for Description
of the Caucasus], vol. 18, pp. 1–26.

Tikhonravov, N 1863, *Pamiatniki Otrechennoy Russkoy Literatury*
[Monuments to the Biblical Apocrypha in Russian
Literature], (in 2 vols.), Published by N Tikhonravov, vol. 1,
Saint Petersburg & vol. 2, Moscow.

Todosiv, V (ed.) 1920, *Sirko*, Vernyhora Association, Kyiv.

Toniev, P 1890, 'Skazki sobrannye v selenii Bayan, Elisavetpolskogo
uezda' [Folk tales collected in the village of Bayan,
Elisabethpol district], *Sbornik Materialov dlia Opisaniya
Kavkaza* [Collection of Materials for Description of the
Caucasus], vol. 9, pp. 184–210.

Ulanowska, S 1884, 'Niektore materyaly etnograficzne we wsi
Lukowen (mazowieckim)' [Some ethnographic materials
from the village of Lukowen (Masovian Voivodeship)],
Zbiór Wiadomości do Antropologii Krajowej [A Collection of
Materials on National Anthropology], vol. 8, pp. 247–323.

Veckenstedt, E 1880, *Wendische Sagen, Märchen und Abergläubische
Gebräuche* [Wendish Sagas, Fairy Tales and Superstitious
Customs], Leuschner & Lubensky Publishing, Graz.

Vereshchagin, G 1886, *Votiaki Sosnovskogo Kraya* [The Udmurts of
Sosnovsky District], (Notes of the Imperial Russian
Geographical Society for the Department of Ethnography,
vol. 14, no. 2), Printing House of the Ministry of Internal
Affairs, Saint Petersburg.

Veselovskiy, A 1868, 'Chr. Schneller: Märchen & Sagen aus Welschtirol:
Ein Beitrag zur deutschen Sagenkunde, 1847' [Chr.
Schneller: Fairy tales & legends from Welschtirol: a
contribution to German legends, 1847], *Zhurnal Ministerstva*

Narodnogo Prosveshcheniya [Journal of the Ministry of Public Education], issue 140, pp. 281–359.

Veselovskiy, A 1880, 'Retsenziya: trudy etnografichesko-statisticheskoy ekspeditsii v Zapadno-Russkiy kray sobrannye Chubinskim' [Review: works of the ethnographic-statistical expedition to the Western Russian (Ukrainian) Lands, collected by Chubynsky], *Otchet o Dvadtsat Vtorom Prisuzhdenii Nagrad Grafa Uvarova* [Report on the Twenty-Second Presentation of Count Uvarov's Awards], Saint Petersburg, pp. 167–230.

Veselovskiy, A 1881, 'Yuzhno-Russkie byliny' [South-Russian (Ukrainian) epics], *Zapiski Imperatorskoy Akademii Nauk: Prilozhenie k Tomu* [Notes of Imperial Academy of Sciences: a Volume Supplement], volume 39, no. 5, pp. 1–78.

Veselovskiy, A 1882, 'Stanislao Prato, la leggenda del tesoro di Rampsinito nelle varie redazioni italiane e straniere, Como, 1882' [Stanislao Prato, the legend of Rampsinito's treasure in the various Italian and foreign versions, Como, 1882], *Zhurnal Ministerstva Narodnogo Prosveshcheniya* [Journal of the Ministry of Public Education], issue 224, pp. 160–166.

Veselovskiy, A 1883, 'Rumänische Märchen übersetzt von Mite Kremnitz, 1882' [Romanian fairy tales translated by Mite Kremnitz, 1882], *Zhurnal Ministerstva Narodnogo Prosveshcheniya* [Journal of the Ministry of Public Education], issue 225, pp. 216–228.

Veselovskiy, A 1886, 'Zametki k istorii apokrifov' [Notes on the history of the Apocrypha], *Zhurnal Ministerstva Narodnogo Prosveshcheniya* [Journal of the Ministry of Public Education], June, pp. 228–302.

Veselovskiy, A 1888, 'Nereshennye, nereshitelnye i bezrazlichnye dantovskogo ada' [Irresolute, indecisive and indifferent ones of Dante's hell] *Zhurnal Ministerstva Narodnogo Prosveshcheniya* [Journal of the Ministry of Public Education], November, pp. 87–116.

Vovk, R (ed.) 1921, *Koza-Dereza: Maliovani Kazky* [Goat-Dereza: Ilustrated Fairy Tales], Dytiacha Bibliotekaka [The Children's Library] Derzhvydav, Odesa.

Vovk, Y (ill.) 1903, *Tsarenko and Zmiy*, Chaika Publishing, Kyiv, Vienna

& Lviv.

Wojcieki, K 1876, *Klechdy, Starozytne Podania i Powiesci Ludowe* [Klechdy, Ancient Legends and Folk Tales], W Drukarni S Lewentala [S Lewental's Printing House], Warsaw.

Wolf, J 1843, *Niederländische Sagen* [Dutch Sagas], Brockhaus, Leipzig.

Yastrebov, V 1894, *Materialy po Etnografii Novorossiyskogo Kraya, Sobrannye v Yelisavetgradskom i Aleksandriyskom Uyezdakh Khersonskoy Gubernii* [Materials on the Ethnography of the Novorossiysk Region, Collected in the Yelysavethrad and Olexandria Counties of the Kherson Province], Tipografiya Okruzhnogo Shtaba, [District Headquarters Printing House], Odesa.

Yakovenko, S (ed.) & Soldatova S (il.) 2018, *The Sparrow and the Bush & The Little Straw Bull*, Sova Books, Sydney.

Yavornytsky, D 1889, 'Pryskazka do nyukharey' [Fable about Sniffers], *Yekaterinoslavskie Gubernskie Vedomosti* [Ekaterinoslav Provincial Gazette], no. 63, August 12, pp. 2–3.

Yefymenko, P 2020, *A Collection of Ukrainian Spells*, Sova Books, Sydney.

Yusbishev, T 1892, 'Armianskaya skazka o semi bratyakh' [The Armenian folk tale about seven brothers], *Sbornik Materialov dlia Opisaniya Kavkaza* [Collection of Materials for Description of the Caucasus], vol. 13, part 2, pp. 323–329.

Zawilinski, R 1889, Z Powieści i Pieśni Górali Beskidowych [From the novels and songs of the Beskid Highlanders], *Bibljoteka Wisły* [Wisla Library], vol. 5, Warsaw.

Zhdanov, I 1893, 'Vasiliy Buslaevich i Volkh Vseslavyevich' [Vasiliy Buslaevich and Volkh Vseslavyevich'], *Zhurnal Ministerstva Narodnogo Prosveshcheniya* [Journal of the Ministry of Public Education], issue 289, pp. 211–264.

Zhytetskyi, P 1893, 'Mysli o Narodnykh Malorusskikh Dumakh' [Thoughts on Ukrainian Folk Dumy], *Kievskaya Starina* [Kyivan Antiquity] Publishing, Kyiv.

Glossary

Baba (plural: *baːby*) – The word has multiple meanings in Ukrainian, including 'old woman'. In this book the word is used in the sense of *znakharka*, see the definition.

Bida – In Ukrainian folklore, this personification of misfortune, poverty, misery, hardship, and grief is often portrayed as a skinny woman dressed in filthy old rags. Once *Bida* finds her victim and settles in their house, it becomes incredibly hard to get rid of her. Her presence is noticed soon after she settles through a series of sudden disasters in the household, such as the house being destroyed by fire or the death of a family member. *Bida* cannot be killed but can be fooled and driven away.

Bohatyr (plural: *bohatyri*) – A hero in folklore, a brave warrior often described as a giant of extraordinary strength and courage. *Bohatyri* are central figures in many epic tales, symbolising the ideal qualities of bravery, strength, and heroism. They frequently embark on quests to protect their people, defeat villains, and uphold justice, reflecting the values and cultural heritage of the societies that created these legends.

Borshch – This traditional Ukrainian soup made with beetroot as the main ingredient, often including cabbage, potatoes, carrots, and meat, served with sour cream.

Bylyna (plural: *bylyny*) – One of the oldest genres of heroic epic poetry of the Ukrainian people, most *bylyny* were created during the times of [Kyivan] Rus. For the most part, they glorify the deeds of historical and folk heroes, including *bohatyri*. The central locations of *bylyny* are Kyiv, Chernihiv, and Novhorod.

Chort (plural: *chorty*) – Also known as 'didko', this mythological evil spirit is a male figure (*chortykha* is the female equivalent). A *chort* can change his appearance, transforming into a man, animal, and so on. Often, a *chort* is portrayed as a man with goat- or ram-like horns, fur, tail, and hooves. Sometimes he even has a snout. Like humans, *chorty* are born, get married, and have children. Their main place of residence is hell, but on earth, *chorty* live in deserted places, at crossroads, and other similar locations. They possess magical powers, which they most often use at night. Their main goal is to harm people and induce them to do something immoral. In Ukrainian folk tales, *chorty* are often depicted as absurd and foolish.

Chumak (plural: *chumaky*) – These 15th to 16th century Ukrainian traders primarily transported salt and fish from the coastal

'Chumaky among the Tumuli' by Taras Shevchenko (1846).

areas of the Black and Azov seas. *Chumaky* were admired and respected by the Ukrainian people for their bravery, as they faced constant dangers from Tatars' and others' attacks during their travels.

Dolia – In Ukrainian folk tales, this personification of fate is exclusively feminine and depicted anthropomorphically often dressed in peasant clothing. It embodies both positive and negative aspects of a person's life, shaped by a combination of supernatural influence and personal actions. While fate is often seen as predetermined and immutable, there are beliefs and narratives suggesting that through certain actions and cunning, one can influence or change their fate.

Domovyk (plural: *domovyky*) – This mythological male figure is a type of house spirit and has no female counterpart. Ukrainian *domovyky* share some similar characteristics with the house spirits of other European countries, such as the 'brownie' in England (sometimes called a 'dobby' in the north). Some legends portray *domovyky* to be just a variety of *chorty*. Others put them into a separate category, presenting their origin as hatching from a tiny egg. It was believed that a *domovyk* settles in the newly built house; and instead of a human, it is he who becomes the master of the house, being involved in the life of the family and running of the household. When everything goes well, there is harmony and love among the family members, domestic animals are well looked after, and, in general, the household is in order – the *domovyk* is pleased, he helps out and, when needed, warns the family of impending danger or misfortune. However, if the *domovyk* is not satisfied with how the home is run or if he is mistreated even by accident, he becomes vicious in his revenge – to the point of burning down the house.

Duma (plural: *dumy*) – This traditional Ukrainian lyrico-epic work of folk origin often narrates historical or cultural events. The *dumy* are not sung, but are rather chanted by a bard to the accompaniment of a bandura, kobza, or lira. *Dumy* are characterised by their rhythmic and melodic structure. *Dumy* typically recount tales of heroism, battles, and the struggles of the Ukrainian people, reflecting their values, beliefs, and historical experiences.

A postcard titled 'Portrait of S. Yashnyi, a Kobzar' by Slastion, 1903, featuring a bandura player.

Had, the Hellish (plural: *hady*) – 'Hellish Serpent' or 'Infernal Reptile'; this mythical creature or demonic entity found in Ukrainian folk tales, is often associated with the underworld (пекло, peklo – hell). This being is typically depicted as a serpent-like or reptilian creature with malevolent powers, symbolising evil and destruction.

Horilka (mass noun) – This Ukrainian distilled spirit has an average 40% alcoholic content. The name *horilka* is derived from the word 'hority,' which means 'to burn'.

Kasha (plural: *kashi*) – A popular Ukrainian dish made from cereals such as buckwheat, barley, and millet. *Kasha* can be prepared with milk or water and can be either sweet or savoury. It is one of the most frequently mentioned dishes in Ukrainian folklore, alongside other traditional foods like *borshch*.

Kolomyika (plural: *kolomyiky*) – This popular form of Ukrainian folk ditty humorously addresses virtually every aspect of everyday life. *Kolomyiky* are found throughout Ukraine, with the Carpathian Hutsul region being considered their heartland. The name is believed to be derived from the Hutsul town of Kolomyia. These ditties are characterised by their lively tempo and rhythmic patterns, often performed with energetic dance moves. *Kolomyiky* often feature improvised, rhymed couplets reflecting themes of love, nature, and humour.

Kotyhoroshko – Also known as *Pokotyhoroshko*, this legendary character in Ukrainian folklore is often depicted as a hero in various

Detail of: Kotyhoroshko: Ukrainian Folk Tales *book cover, featuring Kotyhoroshko; (Milkovytskyi 1975).*

fairy tales and epic stories. *Kotyhoroshko* roughly translates to 'Roll-a-Pea'. The name is derived from the method of his miraculous conception: his mother encountered a rolling pea, picked it up, and ate it. As a result, she became pregnant with *Kotyhoroshko*. He grew up to be a super-strong hero, performing many heroic feats and fighting evil creatures.

Kovbasa (plural: *kovbasy*) – Various kinds of smoked, boiled or fried meat sausages.

Kozhukh (plural: *kozhukhy*) – A long fur coat, usually made from sheepskin, with a large collar and fur on the inside.

Kuma (female; *kum* – male, singular; *kumy*, plural) – This title and form of address is used among the parents and godparents of a baptised child. According to Ukrainian Christian traditions, for a child to be baptised, the child's parents choose a woman and a man to be the child's godparents, i.e., godmother and godfather. The number of a child's godparents varies across Ukraine and, according to the customs of some regions, may reach five or more couples. In Ukraine, while a child calls his or her godparents 'khresnyi tato' (Engl., 'godfather') or 'khresna mama' (Engl., 'godmother'), the child's parents call them 'kum' and 'kuma' and vice versa. Customarily, the relationships among *kumy* become as close as among relatives. It is traditional at least once a year, especially during the Christmas holidays, for a godchild to visit his or her godparents.

Lisovyk (plural: *lisovyky*) – This mythological male figure is a master and protector of the forest: trees, animals and birds. According to some beliefs, *lisovyk* is merely a variety of *chort*. Each *lisovyk* has its own forest and lives in places unreachable by humans. People may see him only when he chooses. Sometimes he is kind and helps people who are lost or assists hunters by sending animals towards them; whereas at other times, especially if the visitors to his forest have no respect for his domain, *lisovyk* can lead them deep into the forest, where they perish.

Mare's Head – This mystical creature from Ukrainian folk tales often appears unexpectedly to challenge the hero. Through these tests, the hero can demonstrate his or her moral virtues. The *Mare's Head* is intimidating and can be harsh to those who show it disrespect. However, for those who pass its test with dignity, it bestows untold wealth and beauty.

Namitka (plural: *namitky*) – This traditional Ukrainian head covering worn by women. It is a long, rectangular piece of cloth, typically made from linen, and it is intricately embroidered or adorned with decorative elements. The *namitka* is wrapped around the head and neck, often with elaborate folds and knots, serving both practical and symbolic purposes.

'Festive attire, Ternopil region, 1932' (Kulchytska 1959, Table 11); featuring a girl in a traditional dress, including namitka *and* sorochka.

Pan (plural: *pany*) – Historically, this honorific was used in Ukraine to address or refer to a rich or noble man, such as a lord or master. In this context, the word *Panych* referred to a young, unmarried man. Today, *Pan* is used before a man's name similarly to the English 'Mr.' The feminine forms of the honorific are *Pani* (English: 'Mrs') and *Panna* (English: 'Ms').

Panych (plural: *panychi*) – In Ukraine, the word *Panych* has a meaning similar to *Pan* but specifically refers to a young, unmarried man or the son of a *Pan* (a title used for nobility or landowners).

Pesyholovets (plural: *pesyholovtsi*) – This mythical anthropomorphic creature in Ukrainian folklore is traditionally described as a one-eyed giant (similar to a cyclops) that devours people. A more modern definition describes them as beings with human bodies and dogs' heads. This definition is based on the morphology of the term 'pesyholovtsi', which is likely derived from the combination of the Ukrainian words 'pes' (dog) and 'holov' ('holova' – head), aligning with the depiction of these creatures having dog-like heads. These beings are often portrayed as fearsome antagonists in various tales.

'The Mistress of the House by the Pich' by Mykhaltseva (in Sketches from Travels across Ukraine, *1882, p. 13).*

Pich (plural: *pechi*) – This brick, clay, or tile structure performed several essential functions in a traditional Ukrainian house: it was used for heating and cooking, and some *pich* designs included an area where one could sit or lie. The cult of the *pich*, as an extension of the cult of fire and the Sun, is manifested in many aspects of Ukrainian culture. The *pich* is included in rituals performed on significant occasions in a person's life: birth (e.g., gently touching a *pich* with a newborn child's or lamb's head); weddings (during a *svatannia* ceremony, a bride-to-be stood timidly at the *pich*, pretending to pick at it); and funerals (e.g., upon returning from the funeral, everyone had to touch the *pich*, symbolising cleansing oneself with fire from the power of the dead). The folk's respect for the *pich* is evident from an old Ukrainian saying, 'I would say [something improper], but there is a *pich* in the house.'

Pokotyhoroshko – see definition of *Kotyhoroshko*.

Propasnytsia (plural: *propasnytsi*) – Also known by various names such as 'triasovytsia', 'triasavytsia', 'triastsia', 'triasets', 'triasuchka', 'khyndia', 'tiotukha', 'zymnytsia', 'vohnevytsia', 'lykhomanka', and 'hariachka'; this term can refer to: (1) fever: including its manifestations such as shivering, shaking, and chills; and (2) mythical creature: a monster that brings fever and death to people. These dual interpretations highlight both the medical and mythological significance of *propasnytsi* in Ukrainian culture.

Salo – A Ukrainian dish, *salo* is cured (salted, brine–fermented or smoked) slabs of pork fatback or pork belly, with little or no meat. *Salo* is usually served as an appetiser or as part of a sandwich; it can also be used as an ingredient in other dishes.

Smert – In Ukrainian folk tale tradition, the character of *Smert* (death) is exclusively feminine. She is entirely anthropomorphic. This character shows no signs of decay and is usually dressed in ordinary peasant clothing. Additionally, the scythe as an attribute is rarely mentioned in these texts. It is assumed that everyone who meets *Smert* recognises her immediately. In the folk tales she can be outwitted or deceived, but temporarily.

Sopilka (plural: *sopilky*) – This traditional Ukrainian musical instrument, akin to a wooden flute. It is an end-blown flute typically made from materials like elder, hazel, reed or other readily available woods.

Sorochka (plural: *sorochky*) – (1) Old-fashioned light loose undergarment, type of a long shirt, with sleeves; or (2) Upper garment, a type of blouse with sleeves; *sorochky* made to be worn on special occasions, were richly embroidered with traditional patterns.

Svat (plural: *svaty*) – see definition of *svatannia*.

Svatannia (mass noun) – An ancient Ukrainian ritual for making or conveying a marriage proposal to a woman. If successful, it initiates a series of ceremonies that constitute a traditional

'Svaty' by Mykola Pymonenko (1882). The image includes the following elements defined in the glossary: pich, starosty, *and* sorochka.

Ukrainian wedding. A brief description of one variation of *svatannia* is as follows: a young woman's suitor comes to her home with his representatives, called *svaty* (singular: *svat*) or *starosty* (singular: *starosta*), to present his marriage proposal. The chief *svat* is usually a relative or close friend of the young man, known for being eloquent and persuasive. The *svaty* are invited to the table, where a discussion resembling bargaining takes place. The *svaty* ask the young woman's parents for their permission to marry their daughter. Even if the parents are willing, they pretend to have doubts and hesitate, creating an opportunity for the *svaty* to convince them. During the ceremony, the young couple stands humbly at a distance: the young woman by the *pich* (see definition) and the young man in the hall. If the *svatannia* is successful, the young woman gives the *svaty* *rushnyky* (traditional embroidered towels) she has made and a kerchief to her suitor. Otherwise, as a sign of refusal, the young man receives a pumpkin. This custom varies across different regions of Ukraine.

Svataty – To make or convey a marriage proposal according to long-established Ukrainian customs. This typically involves a formal ceremony called *svatannia* (see definition), where family members or intermediaries, known as *svaty*, play key roles in negotiating and arranging the marriage proposal. This traditional practice is rich in rituals and symbolism, reflecting the cultural importance of marriage within the community.

Tsar (plural: *tsari*) – In Ukrainian fairy tales, spells, and other forms of folklore, this obsolete title in Eastern Europe refers to a ruler or monarch and is equivalent to the term 'king' used in, for example, British folklore. The *tsar* is often depicted as the sovereign of a vast tsardom, wielding supreme authority and power.

Tsarevych (plural: *tsarevychi*) – This title was historically given to the son or son-in-law of a Tsar. Additionally, a *tsarevych* is a character frequently found in folk tales, often equivalent to a prince in Western and other cultures, undertaking various heroic and adventurous quests.

Tsarivna (plural: *tsrivny*) – This title was given to a Tsar's daughter or daughter-in-law in historical contexts. Additionally, a *tsarivna* is a character often found in folklore, typically depicted as a princess involved in various tales of adventure and romance.

Tsarytsia (plural: *tsarytsi*) – Feminine form of *tsar*, see definition.

Varenyk (plural: *varenyky*) – Also known as 'pyrohy', these are traditional Ukrainian dumplings that can be steamed or boiled, with sweet or savory fillings. Common fillings include meat, *syr* (cheese), potatoes, or various vegetarian options. *Varenyky* can also be fried after boiling to add an additional layer of texture.

Vovkulaka (plural: *vovkulaky*) – In Ukrainian folklore, people, mostly men, who willingly or unwillingly, shape-shift into wolves for some period of time, are called *vovkulaky*. Ukrainian *vovkulaky* are identified with Western European were-wolves. According to a Ukrainian legend, *vovkulaky* are born to the parents, who sinned and indulged in carnal pleasures on forbidden days, such as on the religious holidays or during lent.

Whisper (mass noun) – Ukrainian noun 'shepit' (Engl., 'whisper'), in the context of this book, is a spell incanted by a *znakharka* while performing her healing ritual, such as, rolling an egg or pouring wax. Whisper is usually performed in a monotonous whispering pattern. The verb 'sheptaty' (Engl., 'to whisper') describes the action of performing a whisper.

Zlydni (plural noun) – In Ukrainian mythology and folklore, these are evil spirits that bring misfortune to one's household. *Zlydni* personify poverty. Often *zlydni* are portrayed as small old men in rags. Usually, they live under *pich*. These creatures bring misfortune once they settle in one's house: the family soon falls into poverty. According to the Ukrainian fairy tales, the way to get rid of *zlydni* is to lure them into a bottle, snuffbox, barrel, sack, etc., tie or lock it and throw it away or bury it. Then prosperity would return to the household. However, if another person releases the *zlydni*, they will stick to him and settle in his house. See also *Bida*.

Zmiy (plural: *zmiyi*) – Also, fire *zmiy*, 'letavyts', 'perelet' and 'perelesnyk'; this mythical male creature, a flying fire-breathing giant reptile is the embodiment of an evil spirit, who visits the living. The word 'zmiy' can be translated into English as 'dragon', 'serpent' or 'snake'. The *zmiy* shape-shifts into a handsome man to seduce women in order to drink their blood. In some tales, the *zmiy* appears to a widow in the form of her departed husband. In others, the *zmiy* turns into a golden piece of jewelry or some shiny trinket and entices a young maiden to take it into her possession; in this scenario the *zmiy* also seduces the woman. In most cases the *zmiy* frequently visits his victim, who gradually withers, and if the *zmiy's* visits are not stopped in time, the woman dies.

Zmiya (plural: *zmiyi*) – Translated as 'snake' or 'viper' from Ukrainian, this name refers to a mythical female snake-like creature often depicted as an evil character in Ukrainian folklore. Additionally, in many folk tales, *zmiya* has a daughter who is also malevolent and assists her mother in her wicked deeds. A well-known folk tale featuring *zmiya* is 'Ivasyk-Telesyk'.

Znakhar (plural: *znakhari*) – Also, 'znanyk', 'znatnyk'; a masculane form of *znakharka*, see definition.

Znakharka (plural: *znakharky*) – Also known as 'babka' or 'babka-sheptukha' (English: 'old woman-whisperer' or 'baba-whisperer'), Ukrainian folk healers, *znakharky* (or *znakhari* if men), practice healing through traditional medicine, as opposed to scientific medicine. Their methods may also include the use of prophecy and sorcery. Unlike witches who use black magic, *znakharky* often incorporate Christian prayers and seek help from God and saints in their rituals. *Znakharky* and *znakhari* continue to practise in Ukraine today.

Index 1:

General

Index 2:

Popular Ukrainian Folk Tale Heros and Supernatural Beings

Index 3:
Magic Objects

Magic object	Folk tale no.
boots, the hundred-verst	'1.22. The Son of Shoemaker as the King' on page 41
bulls, a pair of magic (in a single day, the bulls ploughed and levelled an enormous field)	'1.38. The Magic Bulls of the Angel' on page 54
cauldron, palace-conjuring (cauldron, with a knock on which a palace appears)	'1.4. The Magic Stone' on page 25
cloak of twelve soldiers (cloak, from under which twelve soldiers emerge)	'1.4. The Magic Stone' on page 25
flute, the prophetic, see also, *sopilka* & lira	'2.12. About the Murdered Sister' on page 116
handkerchief, golden	'1.75. About the Lazy Son' on page 80
hat of invisibility	'1.2. The Daughter and the Stepdaughter (1)' on page 23
	'1.16. The Treacherous Tsarivna' on page 35
	'1.22. The Son of Shoemaker as the King' on page 41
hen, speckled (or Hen the Riaba; lays precious stones)	'2.5. Hen the Riaba' on page 104
herbs, consuming them grants the ability to understand the language of animals and plants	'2.4. About the Abducted Lad' on page 94
horse that brings forth golden and silver armour from its ears	'1.20. The Glass Mountain' on page 40
lira, the prophetic (see also, flute & *sopilka*)	'2.12. About the Murdered Sister' on page 116
mittens (foam appears from mittens, as a token of distress)	'2.10. About Suchych' on page 102

Magic object	Folk tale no.
pellets, sheep (turn into gold coins)	'1.43. Saint Nicholas and his Shepherds' on page 59
pipe with endless tobacco (pipe-nevykurka)	'2.13. The Pipe-Nevykurka, Purse-Zolotodayka and Sack-Samokhvat' on page 106
purse, gold-giving (purse-zolotodayka)	'2.13. The Pipe-Nevykurka, Purse-Zolotodayka and Sack-Samokhvat' on page 106
ram, gold-horned – produces money	'2.3. About Three Brothers' on page 93
ring, magic (fulfils every wish of its owner)	'1.23. The Merchant and the Tsarivna' on page 44 '2.6. About the Merciful Lad' on page 96
sabre, all-cleaving	'1.16. The Treacherous Tsarivna' on page 35
sack, self-grabbing (sack-samokhvat)	'2.13. The Pipe-Nevykurka, Purse-Zolotodayka and Sack-Samokhvat' on page 106
shirt, indestructible	'1.16. The Treacherous Tsarivna' on page 35
shotgun, infallible	'1.16. The Treacherous Tsarivna' on page 35
shotgun, magic	'1.22. The Son of Shoemaker as the King' on page 41
sopilka that summons grateful animals	'1.13 & 1.14. The Insidious Sister' on page 32
sopilka, when played everyone is forced to dance	'2.33. About the Priest's Hireling' on page 130
staff, water-parting	'1.2. The Daughter and the Stepdaughter (1)' on page 23
stick, self-beating (stick-samobiy)	'1.22. The Son of Shoemaker as the King' on page 41 '1.75. About the Lazy Son' on page 80 '2.3. About Three Brothers' on page 93 '1.4. The Magic Stone' on page 25
stone, magic (transforms into a table laden with food and drinks)	'1.4. The Magic Stone' on page 25
table that supplies all kinds of food (see also, stone turns into a table full of food and drinks)	'1.75. About the Lazy Son' on page 80 '2.3. About Three Brothers' on page 93

Magic object	Folk tale no.
wagon, covering-hundred-mile	'1.2. The Daughter and the Stepdaughter (1)' on page 23
wand, magic (builds a palace)	'1.75. About the Lazy Son' on page 80
water, life-giving	'1.13 & 1.14. The Insidious Sister' on page 32
	'1.17. The Zmiy-Slayer' on page 36
	'2.5. Hen the Riaba' on page 104
water, youth-giving	'1.12. The Youth-Giving Water' on page 31
whip (blood appearing on the whip as a token of distress)	'2.10. About Suchych' on page 102

Index 4:

Impossible Tasks

Impossible tasks	Folk tale no.
to arrive both riding and yet not riding, naked but wearing a *sorochka*, with a gift and yet without one	'2.26. Hurka, the Seven-Year-Old Girl' on page 121
to build a golden bridge	'1.28. Return of the Father's Promissory Note' on page 43
to carry *Zmiy* (Dragon) over the threshold, cook him supper, wash his head, make his bed, and ring the bell over his head all night (to be completed by a girl)	'2.9. The Wicked Stepmother and Her Daughter' on page 101
to drain the sea (and to fell the entire forest; plough the field, sow and reap wheat) in one day	'1.1. The King's Son and the Chort's Daughter' on page 21
to drink twelve barrels of beer	'1.18. The King's Daughter and the Shepherd' on page 37
to eat twelve cows	'1.18. The King's Daughter and the Shepherd' on page 37
to fell a forest	'1.2. The Daughter and the Stepdaughter (1)' on page 23
to fell the entire forest (and to drain the sea; plough the field, sow and reap wheat) in one day	'1.1. The King's Son and the Chort's Daughter' on page 21
to hatch chicks from fifteen baked eggs	'2.26. Hurka, the Seven-Year-Old Girl' on page 121
to kill *Zmiyi* (cf dragons)	'1.18. The King's Daughter and the Shepherd' on page 37
to make a loom from twigs	'2.26. Hurka, the Seven-Year-Old Girl' on page 121
to obtain a golden bird	'1.21. The Golden Bird and the Sea Tsarivna' on page 40
to obtain a golden horse	'1.21. The Golden Bird and the Sea Tsarivna' on page 40

Impossible tasks	Folk tale no.
to obtain a mountain of gold	'1.18. The King's Daughter and the Shepherd' on page 37
to obtain flour from a *chort's* (devil's) mill	'1.13 & 1.14. The Insidious Sister' on page 32
to obtain milk from a hare, a wolf, and a bear	'1.13 & 1.14. The Insidious Sister' on page 32
to obtain the Sea Tsarytsia	'1.21. The Golden Bird and the Sea Tsarivna' on page 40
to plough the field, sow and reap wheat (and to fell the entire forest and to drain the sea) in one day	'1.1. The King's Son and the Chort's Daughter' on page 21
to pose a riddle to the Tsarivna that she could not solve	'2.25. The Riddle-Tale' on page 132
to shepherd ten hares	'1.18. The King's Daughter and the Shepherd' on page 37
to sleep on hot iron	'1.18. The King's Daughter and the Shepherd' on page 37
to sow a field	'1.2. The Daughter and the Stepdaughter (1)' on page 23
to sow cooked millet (millet *kasha*)	'2.26. Hurka, the Seven-Year-Old Girl' on page 121
to spin 100 ells of cloth from a handful of yarn	'2.26. Hurka, the Seven-Year-Old Girl' on page 121
to tame a horse	'1.28. Return of the Father's Promissory Note' on page 43
to tell a tall tale to an old man without him uttering the words, 'You are lying.'	'2.29. About the Wise Simpleton' on page 138

Index 5:

Numbers

No.	Example	Folk tale no.
1	one daughter (and seven sons)	'2.26. Hurka, the Seven-Year-Old Girl' on page 121
2	two bowls of coins	'1.20. The Glass Mountain' on page 39
2	two roosters	'1.34. How the Young Man Made the Rich Maiden Laugh' on page 47
2	two rams	'1.34. How the Young Man Made the Rich Maiden Laugh' on page 47
2	two brothers	'1.40. Two Brothers' on page 56
2	two brothers	'1.47. The Rich Man and the Poor Man' on page 65
2	two coins	'1.76. A Fairy Tale about a Clever Furrier' on page 83
2	two brothers	'2.16. About the Rich Man in a Village' on page 113
2	two comrades	'2.20. About Two Comrades and the Wicked Wife' on page 117
2	two brothers	'2.26. Hurka, the Seven-Year-Old Girl' on page 121
3	chort's three daughters	'1.1. The King's Son and the Chort's Daughter' on page 21
3	three sons	'1.12. The Youth-Giving Water' on page 31
3	three daughters	'1.17. The Zmiy-Slayer' on page 36
3	three trials	'1.19. The Shoemaker and the Bear' on page 38
3	three sons	'1.20. The Glass Mountain' on page 39
3	three hairs	'1.20. The Glass Mountain' on page 39
3	three sons	'1.21. The Golden Bird and the Sea Tsarivna' on page 40
3	three sons	'1.43. Saint Nicholas and his Shepherds' on page 59
3	three years	'1.44. Three Pieces of Advice' on page 58
3	three pieces of advice	'1.44. Three Pieces of Advice' on page 58

No.	Example	Folk tale no.
3	three brothers	'1.46. Punished Greed' on page 64
3	three riddles	'1.49. Three Riddles' on page 66
3	three brothers	'1.57. Three Brothers' on page 70
3	three sons	'1.58. Three Sons' on page 71
3	three sons	'1.59. The Fortunate Purchase' on page 72
3	three brothers	'1.60. The Fortunate Sale' on page 72
3	three lovers of one woman	'1.65. The Husband and Three Lovers of his Wife' on page 72
3	three peas	'1.75. About the Lazy Son' on page 82
3	three brothers	'2.2. About the Fortunate Fool' on page 101
3	three brothers (sons)	'2.3. About Three Brothers' on page 103
3	three times (a dove landed on a future Tsar's head)	'2.5. Hen the Riaba' on page 104
3	three helpful animals	'2.6. About the Merciful Lad' on page 98
3	three sisters	'2.10. About Suchych' on page 104
3	three sisters	'2.12. About the Murdered Sister' on page 107
3	three months	'2.14. About Iohan the Tsar' on page 120
3	three young men	'2.15. About the Chumak's Daughter' on page 112
3	three brides (maidens)	'2.15. About the Chumak's Daughter' on page 112
3	three robbers	'2.17. About the Robbers' on page 114
3	three *Propasnytsi* [Fevers]	'2.23. About the Propasnytsia and the Peasant' on page 120
3	three brothers	'2.29. About the Wise Simpleton' on page 127
4	four oxen	'1.37. Tymko the Thief and the Chorty' on page 50
4	four rubles	'1.62. The Thief in Confession' on page 73
4	four times (a deceased was buried)	'1.69. The Old Woman, who was Buried Four Times' on page 75
4	four crows	'2.25. The Riddle-Tales' on page 122
7	seven years (Tsar's son was ill for)	'1.5 & 1.6 He, who was Born under a Lucky Star' on page 26
7	seven years (Tsar's son was ill for)	'1.5 & 1.6 He, who was Born under a Lucky Star' on page 26
7	seven grains	'1.34. How the Young Man Made the Rich Maiden Laugh' on page 47

No.	Example	Folk tale no.
7	seven sons (and one daughter)	'2.26. Hurka, the Seven-Year-Old Girl' on page 121
7	seven-year-old Hurka	'2.26. Hurka, the Seven-Year-Old Girl' on page 121
8	eight coins	'1.76. A Fairy Tale about a Clever Furrier' on page 83
9	nine-headed *Zmiy*	'2.10. About Suchych' on page 102
9	nine metal doors	'2.10. About Suchych' on page 102
10	ten hares to shepherd	'1.18. The King's Daughter and the Shepherd' on page 37
11	eleven maidens (sisters)	'1.32. The Chort and the Bread' on page 46
11	eleven young men (brothers)	'1.32. The Chort and the Bread' on page 46
12	twelve soldiers	'1.4. The Magic Stone' on page 25
12	twelve brothers	'1.11. The Substitution' on page 30
12	twelve maidens	'1.11. The Substitution' on page 30
12	twelve robbers	'1.13 & 1.14. The Insidious Sister' on page 32
12	twelve cows to eat	'1.18. The King's Daughter and the Shepherd' on page 37
12	twelve barrels of beer	'1.18. The King's Daughter and the Shepherd' on page 37
12	twelfth brother	'1.32. The Chort and the Bread' on page 46
12	twelve children	'2.24. About Baba the Whisperer' on page 120
12	twelve robbers	'2.25. The Riddle-Tale' on page 138
13	13-weeks-old Vasyl the Tsarevych	'1.17. The Zmiy-Slayer' on page 36
15	fifteen baked eggs	'2.26. Hurka, the Seven-Year-Old Girl' on page 121
15	fifteen rubles	'2.31. Kyryk' on page 129
20	twenty years	'1.45. Adventures of the Foundling' on page 59
30	thirty years	'1.39. The Judgment of God' on page 53
50	fifty lashes	'2.18. What is Destined to Someone, it will Be' on page 116
100	100 ells of cloth	'2.26. Hurka, the Seven-Year-Old Girl' on page 121
100	100 rubles	'2.32. About Ivan the Priest's Hireling' on page 142
300	300 years	'1.42. About the Priest, who Slept in Heaven for Three Hundred Years' on page 58

Index 6:

Shape-Shifting Forms

Form	Shape-shifter	Folk tale no.
cat	hero	'1.18. The King's Daughter and the Shepherd' on page 37
cross	hero (King's son)	'1.1. The King's Son and the Chort's Daughter' on page 21
deer, the golden-horned	angel	'2.14. About Iohan the Tsar' on page 110
donkey	Tsarytsia (Tsar turned his wife into a donkey as punisment)	'2.5. Hen the Riaba' on page 95
drake	hero (cabman)	'1.16. The Treacherous Tsarivna' on page 35
drake	hero	'1.28. Return of the Father's Promissory Note' on page 43
duck	the drowned woman transformed into a duck; when the duck was killed, she became two golden trees. When the trees were cut down, she fell as a sliver and turned back into a woman	'2.8. Brother the Little Ram' on page 98
horse, golden	hero (cabman)	'1.16. The Treacherous Tsarivna' on page 35
leaves, golden	hero (cabman)	'1.16. The Treacherous Tsarivna' on page 35
lightning	supernatural / demonic being (*chort*)	'1.1. The King's Son and the Chort's Daughter' on page 21
maiden	the strings of the lira transformed back into the murdered maiden, who had been killed by her sisters	'2.12. About the Murdered Sister' on page 105
maiden	dog	'2.15. About the Chumak's Daughter' on page 112

Form	Shape-shifter	Folk tale no.
maiden	pig	'2.15. About the Chumak's Daughter' on page 112
millet	supernatural / demonic being (Lucifer's youngest daughter)	'1.28. Return of the Father's Promissory Note' on page 43
mouse	magic object (youth-giving water)	'1.12. The Youth-Giving Water' on page 31
pillar	hero (King's son)	'1.1. The King's Son and the Chort's Daughter' on page 21
pillar	Tsarivna turned her husband into a pillar; he then turned her into a pillar as punishment	'2.6. About the Merciful Lad' on page 106
ram	the brother drank the water and turned into a little ram	'2.8. Brother the Little Ram' on page 98
rat	magic object (youth-giving water)	'1.12. The Youth-Giving Water' on page 31
sea	supernatural being (*chort's* daughter)	'1.1. The King's Son and the Chort's Daughter' on page 21
thunder	supernatural being (*chort*)	'1.1. The King's Son and the Chort's Daughter' on page 21
tree, apple	hero (cabman)	'1.16. The Treacherous Tsarivna' on page 35
tree, apple	supernatural / demonic being (*Zmiy's* wife)	'1.18. The King's Daughter and the Shepherd' on page 37
tree, pine	supernatural / demonic being (*Zmiy's* wife)	'1.18. The King's Daughter and the Shepherd' on page 37
trees, two golden,	the drowned woman transformed into a duck; when the duck was killed, she became two golden trees. When the trees were cut down, she fell as a sliver and turned back into a woman	'2.8. Brother the Little Ram' on page 98
water	supernatural / demonic being (*chort's* daughter)	'1.1. The King's Son and the Chort's Daughter' on page 21
water	supernatural / demonic being (Lucifer's youngest daughter)	'1.28. Return of the Father's Promissory Note' on page 43
well	supernatural / demonic being (*Zmiy's* wife)	'1.18. The King's Daughter and the Shepherd' on page 37
wheat	hero	'1.28. Return of the Father's Promissory Note' on page 43

Index 7:

Punishment and Execution Methods

Method	Description	Folk tale no.
a series of punishments	following a bet, a hireling slaughtered the priest's oxen, killed his dog and children, drowned his wife, and cut off the priest's beard, ultimately receiving 100 rubles from him	'2.32. About Ivan the Priest's Hireling' on page 148
a series of punishments	the merchant, acting on his wife's false accusations, cut off his sister's arms and cast her into a pit	'1.8. The Envious Wife' on page 28
beheading	the brother beheaded his sister and her lover for plotting to kill him	'1.13 & 1.14. The Insidious Sister' on page 32
beheading	the husband beheaded his wife and her lover as punishment for their attempt to kill him	'1.16. The Treacherous Tsarivna' on page 35
drawing and quartering	two villains were drawn and quartered by horses for harming the Tsarivna and her son	'1.9. The Virtuous Daughter and Wife' on page 29
drawing and quartering	the Tsar transformed his murderous sister-in-law into a donkey and subsequently had her dismembered by horses in the field as punishment for killing his brother	'2.5. Hen the Riaba' on page 95
drawing and quartering	the Pan ordered the dismemberment of his wife's maid, the murderous imposter, by horses in the field as punishment for killing his wife	'2.8. Brother the Little Ram' on page 98
entombing	the king's son immured the impostor (evil maiden) within a wall for deceiving him	'1.2. The Daughter and the Stepdaughter (1)' on page 23
entombing	the Tsarevych immured the merchant's envious wife within a wall	'1.8. The Envious Wife' on page 28

execution	the grandsons executed their grandmother and her lover as punishment for their attempt to kill the grandsons' father	'1.17. The Zmiy-Slayer' on page 36
exile	the Tsarevych exiled his wife based on the false accusations made by the merchant's wife	'1.8. The Envious Wife' on page 28
exile	the king exiled his daughter for becoming pregnant out of wedlock	'1.17. The Zmiy-Slayer' on page 36
exile	the tsar exiled his daughter for becoming pregnant out of wedlock	'1.75. About the Lazy Son' on page 80
flogging	the *Pan* ordered his servants to administer 50 lashes to a peasant as punishment for accidentally killing his bird	'2.18. What Is Destined Will Come to Pass' on page 126
hanging	the Tsarivna's husband, revealed to be a robber and murderer, was hanged for his crimes	'1.15. The Robber and the Tsarivna' on page 34
incarceration	two sisters were imprisoned for killing their third sister, who later returned to life	'2.12. About the Murdered Sister' on page 107
incarceration	God placed the soldier in the sack-samokhvat (self-grabbing sack) until the Last Judgment, as retribution for the soldier having done the same to Apostle Peter	'2.13. The Pipe-Nevykurka, Purse-Zolotodayka and Sack-Samokhvat' on page 106
killing (as a crime)	the merchant ordered the execution of his daugher, demanding her little finger and heart as proof of her death	'1.9. The Virtuous Daughter and Wife' on page 29
killing (as a crime)	the father ordered the execution of his youngest son, demanding his little finger and heart as proof of his death	'1.12. The Youth-Giving Water' on page 31
supernatural affliction	toads and snakes poured from the evil maiden's eyes and mouth as punishment for her greed	'1.2. The Daughter and the Stepdaughter (1)' on page 23
thrashing	the husband gave a thrashing to his wife for scolding and beating him for a period of time.	'2.20. About Two Comrades and the Wicked Wife' on page 127

torture (as a crime)	following a bet, a hireling slaughtered the priest's oxen, killed his dog and children, drowned his wife, and cut off the priest's beard, ultimately receiving 100 rubles from him	'2.29. About the Wise Simpleton' on page 138
transforming someone into an animal or object	the Tsar transformed his murderous sister-in-law into a donkey and subsequently had her dismembered by horses in the field as punishment for killing his brother	'2.5. Hen the Riaba' on page 95
transforming someone into an animal or object	the husband transformed his wife, the Tsarivna, into a pillar but later restored her to human form as retribution for her having first turned him into a pillar	'2.6. About the Merciful Lad' on page 98

Index 8:

Folk Tale
Recording Locations

Kolberg's Collection		
Geographical name – Modern	Folk tale no.	Geographical name as cited in the original (Kolberg 1882–89, vol. 4)
Chortovets village	1.5	Chortovets
Chortovets village	1.7	Near Obertyn (Chortovets)
Chortovets village	1.10	Chortovets
Chortovets village	1.14	Chortovets and Unizh
Chortovets village	1.37	Chortovets
Chortovets village	1.55	Chortovets
Chortovets village	1.68	Obertyn, Chortovets
Herasymiv village	1.4	Nezvysko and Herasymiv
Horodenka town	1.8	Near Horodenka (Strilche)
Horodenka town	1.9	Horodenka
Horodenka town	1.12	Near Horodenka
Horodenka town	1.16	Near Horodenka
Horodenka town	1.20	Near Horodenka (Horodnytsia)
Horodenka town	1.21	Near Horodenka (Potochyshche)
Horodenka town	1.22	Near Horodenka (Horodnytsia)
Horodenka town	1.24	Near Horodenka (Horodnytsia)
Horodenka town	1.25	Near Horodenka (Yaseniv-Pilnyi)
Horodenka town	1.28	Near Horodenka (Horodnytsia)
Horodenka town	1.29	Near Horodenka (Horodnytsia)
Horodenka town	1.30	Near Horodenka

Kolberg's Collection		
Geographical name – Modern	Folk tale no.	Geographical name as cited in the original (Kolberg 1882–89, vol. 4)
Horodenka town	1.33	Near Horodenka (Strilche)
Horodenka town	1.38	Near Horodenka (Horodnytsia)
Horodenka town	1.40	Near Horodenka
Horodenka town	1.42	Near Horodenka
Horodenka town	1.44	Near Horodenka
Horodenka town	1.47	Near Horodenka (Soroky)
Horodenka town	1.50	Near Horodenka (Horodnytsia)
Horodenka town	1.52	Near Horodenka (Yaseniv-Pilnyi)
Horodenka town	1.59	Near Horodenka
Horodenka town	1.62	Near Horodenka
Horodenka town	1.63	Near Horodenka
Horodenka town	1.64	Near Horodenka
Horodenka town	1.66	Near Horodenka
Horodenka town	1.69	Near Horodenka
Horodenka town	1.71	Near Horodenka
Horodenka town	1.72	Near Horodenka
Horodnytsia village	1.20	Near Horodenka (Horodnytsia)
Horodnytsia village	1.22	Near Horodenka (Horodnytsia)
Horodnytsia village	1.24	Near Horodenka (Horodnytsia)
Horodnytsia village	1.28	Near Horodenka (Horodnytsia)
Horodnytsia village	1.29	Near Horodenka (Horodnytsia)
Horodnytsia village	1.38	Near Horodenka (Horodnytsia)
Horodnytsia village	1.50	Near Horodenka (Horodnytsia)
Hvizdets town	1.18	Hvizdets, Soroky
Hvizdets town	1.26	Hvizdets
Hvizdets town	1.31	Hvizdets
Hvizdets town	1.32	Near Hvizdets
Hvizdets town	1.39	Hvizdets

Kolberg's Collection		
Geographical name – Modern	Folk tale no.	Geographical name as cited in the original (Kolberg 1882–89, vol. 4)
Hvizdets town	1.51	Hvizdets
Hvizdets town	1.61	Hvizdets
Iltsi village	1.73	Zhabye–Iltsi
Iltsi village	1.74	Zhabye–Iltsi
Iltsi village	1.75	Zhabye–Iltsi
Iltsi village	1.76	Zhabye–Iltsi
Iltsi village	1.77	Zhabye–Iltsi
Khotymyr village	1.2.	Near Obertyn (Khotymyr)
Kliuchiv [Velykyi Klyuchiv] village	1.34	Spas and Kliuchiv villages
Kliuchiv [Velykyi Klyuchiv] village	1.36	Near Kolomyia (Kliuchiv)
Kolomyia town	1.1.	Near Kolomyia (Spas and Myshyn)
Kolomyia town	1.35	Near Kolomyia (Pyadyky)
Kolomyia town	1.36	Near Kolomyia (Kliuchiv)
Kolomyia town	1.46	Near Kolomyia (Yabluniv)
Kolomyia town	1.53	Near Kolomyia (Verbyazh)
Kolomyia town	1.54	Kolomyia
Kolomyia town	1.56	Kolomyia
Kolomyia town	1.67	Near Kolomyia (Turka)
Kulachkivtsi village	1.11	Kulachkivtsi, Zahaipil
Kulachkivtsi village	1.41	Kulachkivtsi
Kulachkivtsi village	1.43	Kulachkivtsi
Kulachkivtsi village	1.49	Kulachkivtsi
Kulachkivtsi village	1.57	Kulachkivtsi
Kulachkivtsi village	1.58	Kulachkivtsi
Myshyn village	1.1.	Near Kolomyia (Spas and Myshyn)
Myshyn village	1.3	Spas and Myshyn
Myshyn village	1.6	Spas and Myshyn

Kolberg's Collection

Geographical name – Modern	Folk tale no.	Geographical name as cited in the original (Kolberg 1882–89, vol. 4)
Myshyn village	1.13	Spas and Myshyn
Myshyn village	1.19	Spas and Myshyn
Myshyn village	1.23	Spas and Myshyn
Myshyn village	1.27	Near Kolomyia (Spas and Myshyn)
Myshyn village	1.70	Spas and Myshyn
Nezvysko village	1.4	Nezvysko and Herasymiv
Obertyn village	1.2.	Near Obertyn (Khotymyr)
Obertyn village	1.7	Near Obertyn (Chortovets)
Obertyn village	1.15	Near Obertyn
Obertyn village	1.68	Obertyn, Chortovets
Potochyshche village	1.21	Near Horodenka (Potochyshche)
Pyadyky village	1.35	Near Kolomyia (Pyadyky)
Pyadyky village	1.60	Pyadyky
Sniatyn town	1.65	Near Sniatyn
Soroky village	1.18	Hvizdets, Soroky
Soroky village	1.47	Near Horodenka (Soroky)
Spas village	1.1.	Near Kolomyia (Spas and Myshyn)
Spas village	1.3	Spas and Myshyn
Spas village	1.6	Spas and Myshyn
Spas village	1.13	Spas and Myshyn
Spas village	1.19	Spas and Myshyn
Spas village	1.23	Spas and Myshyn
Spas village	1.27	Near Kolomyia (Spas and Myshyn)
Spas village	1.34	Spas and Kliuchiv villages
Spas village	1.70	Spas and Myshyn
Strilche village	1.8	Near Horodenka (Strilche)
Strilche village	1.33	Near Horodenka (Strilche)
Tlumach town	1.17	Near Tlumach

Kolberg's Collection		
Geographical name – Modern	Folk tale no.	Geographical name as cited in the original (Kolberg 1882–89, vol. 4)
Turka village	1.67	Near Kolomyia (Turka)
Unizh village	1.14	Chortovets and Unizh
Unknown	1.45	
Verbyazh village	1.53	Near Kolomyia (Verbyazh)
Yabluniv village	1.46	Near Kolomyia (Yabluniv)
Yaseniv-Pilnyi village	1.25	Near Horodenka (Yaseniv-Pilnyi)
Yaseniv-Pilnyi village	1.52	Near Horodenka (Yaseniv-Pilnyi)
Zahaipil village	1.11	Kulachkivtsi, Zahaipil
Zhabye village	1.73	Zhabye–Iltsi
Zhabye village	1.74	Zhabye–Iltsi
Zhabye village	1.75	Zhabye–Iltsi
Zhabye village	1.76	Zhabye–Iltsi
Zhabye village	1.77	Zhabye–Iltsi

Moszynska's Collection		
Geographical name	Folk tale no.	Comments
Cherepyn village (Tarashcha county)	2.16	Recorded from a man, peasant.
Cherkasy village near Ozirna village (Vasylkiv county)	'the rest [of the folk tales]' (Moszynska 1885, p. 160)	Recorded from Marta Bubenchykha, a 70-year-old woman.
Nastashky village (Tarashcha county)	'most of the folk tales' (Moszynska 1885, p. 160)	Recorded from Hapka Tsarenkova, an old woman, a famous storyteller in the whole area.
Tkhorivka village (Skvyra county)	2.4 & 2.11	Recorded from a woman.

Editorial Note

This book is part of the *Ukrainian Scholar Library* series, a collection of academic writings on a broad range of topics by Ukrainian scholars over the centuries.

This is the first English translation of Mykola Sumtsov's review of two Polish collections of the Ukrainian folk tales (Sumtsov 1894c).

We use words 'Ukraine' and 'Ukrainians' instead of 'Malorosiya' [Little Russia] and 'Malorosy' [Little Russians], which were used in the original text. Ukrainian personal and geographical names are transliterated to reflect their correct spelling and pronunciation in Ukrainian.

Our indexes, such as the 'Index 4: Impossible Tasks' on page 203, are based on Sumtsov's summaries of the folk tales rather than their full versions as published by Kolberg (1882–89, vol. 4) and Moszynska (1885).

While Mykola Sumtsov's writings are undoubtedly outstanding and notable (see also our publication of his article in Sumtsov 2019), his references are frequently incomplete or inaccurate. We have endeavoured to provide full details for most of these references. In cases where we were unable to locate sources, we have noted this in our footnotes.

The text has been extensively edited. Where necessary, footnotes or comments have been added to explain editorial changes. Any words or phrases in square brackets throughout the text were added by the translator unless otherwise indicated.

The words 'Ukraine' ('Ukrainian') and 'Poland' ('Polish') appear frequently throughout the text and are therefore not listed as separate entries in the index.

The Glossary includes terms that lack direct English equivalents or carry specific cultural connotations important to the context.

Since the book is printed in black and white, some illustrations have been digitally enhanced to improve the visibility of essential details.

Sova Books

Ukrainian Scholar Library

Published

The Story of Pysanka: a Collection of Articles on Ukrainian Easter Eggs
Mykola Sumtsov, Vasyl Horlenko, Matviy Nomys and Others

A Collection of Ukrainian Spells
Petro Yefymenko

Notes on Ukrainian Demonology
Vasyl Myloradovych

Coming Soon

The Cure Beneath Our Feet
Yuriy Lypa

Ukrainian Folk Worldview: A Sketch of Ukrainian Mythology
Ivan Nechui-Levytskyi

www.ingramcontent.com/pod-product-compliance
Lightning Source LLC
Chambersburg PA
CBHW072129270326
41931CB00010B/1716